PALMERSTON
AND THE HUNGARIAN
REVOLUTION

T0382287

C. Sproxton

PALMERSTON
AND THE HUNGARIAN
REVOLUTION

A DISSERTATION WHICH WAS AWARDED
THE PRINCE CONSORT PRIZE
1914

BY

CHARLES SPROXTON, B.A., M.C.

CAPTAIN, YORKSHIRE REGIMENT
FELLOW OF PETERHOUSE

CAMBRIDGE
AT THE UNIVERSITY PRESS
1919

CAMBRIDGE
UNIVERSITY PRESS

University Printing House, Cambridge CB2 8BS, United Kingdom

Cambridge University Press is part of the University of Cambridge.

It furthers the University's mission by disseminating knowledge in the pursuit of
education, learning and research at the highest international levels of excellence.

www.cambridge.org
Information on this title: www.cambridge.org/9781107511521

© Cambridge University Press 1919

First published 1919
First paperback edition 2015

A catalogue record for this publication is available from the British Library

ISBN 978-1-107-51152-1 Paperback

PREFATORY NOTE

THE PRINCE CONSORT PRIZE (founded in 1883 from the Prince Consort Memorial Fund) was awarded in 1914 to Arthur William Tedder, B.A. of Magdalene, and Charles Sproxton, B.A. of Peterhouse. Charles Sproxton's Dissertation, which follows, has been printed, in accordance with the Regulations, at the expense of the University. But the Syndics of the Press have kindly allowed a Memoir of Captain Sproxton, contributed to *The Cambridge Review* by his tutor and friend, Captain H. W. V. Temperley, Fellow of his College, to be prefixed to the Essay, and I have added a few biographical data. The Syndics have, also, allowed the reproduction of an excellent photograph of our late Junior Fellow, found among his books, which have been placed as a memorial of him in our College Library. We have to thank the Editor of *The Cambridge Review* for allowing the reprint of the Memoir. And I desire also to express my gratitude to Dr J. Holland Rose, University Reader in Modern History, who acted as Examiner for the Prince Consort Prize in 1914, for allowing me, in looking through the Dissertation for the Press, to refer to the valuable MS notes made by him in the course of his reading it. No attempt has been made to introduce any alteration into text or footnotes, except where there could be no doubt that it would have had the immediate assent of the writer of the Essay. Even his invariable use of 'English' and 'England'—where 'British' and 'Great Britain' would have been more correct—has not been changed. The German quotations I have thought it advisable to translate into English. More important alterations or enlargements it seemed best to forego, so that this essay might remain entirely the work of the historical scholar whom we have lost and of whom it must form the only memorial in print. His friends had reason for hoping that he might have a share in the writing of the history of the present war; but he has died as one of its heroes.

A. W. W.

Peterhouse,
All Souls' Day, 1918.

CHARLES SPROXTON

CHARLES, the son of Mr Arthur Sproxton, now of Lee Street, Holderness Road, Hull, and formerly of Salt End, Medon, was born in 1890, and educated at the Municipal (Boulevard) School, Hull, where he twice won the Royal Geographical Society's Medal. He entered into residence at Peterhouse in October, 1909, with an East Riding Major Scholarship, and obtained, soon after, a College Exhibition in History, to which study he had from the first resolved to devote himself. His Tutor in History was Mr H. W. V. Temperley, Fellow and Assistant Tutor of the College. In 1911 he gained a Foundation Scholarship, and, having in the same year obtained a First Class in Part I of the Historical Tripos and followed this up with another First Class in Part II of the same Tripos in 1912, graduated B.A. and was appointed a Hugo de Balsham (Research) Student of the College. He had carried off the Gladstone Memorial Prize, and in 1914 he obtained one of the Prince Consort Memorial prizes.

Charles Sproxton, who was in the O.T.C. at Cambridge, received his first commission within a month after the declaration of war. He was promoted Lieutenant in Alexandra and Princess of Wales's Own Yorkshire Regiment in April, 1915, and Captain in June, 1916. He was twice wounded—in May, 1915 and in June, 1916—and was mentioned in despatches in November, 1915, having previously received the Military Cross for conspicuous gallantry and resource, in July and August of that year, at Walverghem and near Armentieres. He came home on sick leave in the summer of 1916, and returned to active service as Adjutant of his Battalion. He fell on July 19th, 1917, at the Western Front.

The younger historians have suffered as much as or more than almost any other branch of learning at Cambridge. At least it is striking to think that a small society of twelve resident members is now reduced by one half. It were an invidious task to say which of these is most missed, but certainly there was an end to bright promise of achievement when Charles Sproxton died.

He was interesting because he passed through life with a sort of mild serenity, always wondering but never astonished at what it brought him. Born and bred in Yorkshire, accustomed from birth to the wild moors round his native home and to the stern objectivity of northern character, he was suddenly translated to Cambridge. He came up with a County Council Scholarship and very soon developed historical gifts of remarkable power. The word 'developed' is perhaps misleading; for his mind resembled a cave, which revealed something that was hidden, if you penetrated it in the right way. He did not give the teacher the idea of developing intellect or imagination, but of revealing it. His power of observation was not trained or expanded by his study—study simply enabled scales to fall from his eyes. He obtained a first in both parts of the Historical Tripos, and was Hugo de Balsham Research Scholar at Peterhouse, Gladstone and Prince Consort Prizeman and finally Fellow of his College. There was a sort of mild inevitability about his success which surprised those who did not know him well, but which his friends perfectly understood.

His characteristics were those of a nature shy and retiring to outward view, but intense and imaginative within. The freedom and joy of college life appealed to him, for he breathed an air and a life which he had not hitherto known and to which his nature instinctively responded. In pure historical work he made his mark by a fellowship dissertation on the Hungarian Revolution of 1848, on its diplomatic side, to write which he delved deep in the records; among other things, he discovered that a German book professedly based on the British records, which had deceived at least one distinguished British historian, was a forgery. His forecast was afterwards verified and accepted by the Record Office, and characteristically he neither claimed nor received any credit for the discovery. His essay was marked by sound research, historic grasp and a real eye for diplomatic motive. Like all young men's work it offered itself to criticism on some sides, but it was a study of extraordinary promise and undoubted originality. It deserves to be published and, if it is, will fill a gap in our knowledge of the Palmerstonian epoch.

Yet, though he possessed rare historical attainments, I believe that the chief influences upon him were literary and religious. His imagination was almost medieval in its wealth and in its simplicity. Francis Thompson was his King of Poets, who had said the last word in imagery and style. Indeed this writer appealed to him in his moods of mysticism, as well as by his manner. Unquestionably his own style and thought were thus greatly influenced, and a series of sonnets which he wrote, though full of originality, bears unmistakable traces of Thompson. In the same way the Anglican Church, with its medieval and mystic traditions, appealed to him as did the Catholic to Thompson. Father Figgis was one of those who, both by writings and personal intercourse, had the deepest influence upon him. He was one who loved mysticism for its own sake, just as he loved style. Words which flushed and glowed or fell like music, a faith which burned and thrilled, these were part of his emotional nature.

His dreamy temperament led him to pensiveness and reflection, and one hardly thought of him as capable of action. Yet those who knew him best could again have told a tale. When on a visit to the Lakes he astonished all his companions by his physical endurance, as afterwards in the trenches he bore hardships without a murmur, perhaps almost without realising that they were such. There were those, too, who heard him speak in the college societies, who knew that his nature contained unexpected fires. Those who heard it will never forget one speech, in which he spoke of Mohammedanism as "the religion I reverence most after my own," or a meeting at the Historical Society in which he poured scorn on the doctrine that "nothing succeeds like success." Thus it was that, when the war came, he had no doubt about his choice. He did not enlist, as some did, because it was a duty, but because he considered it a privilege. In his eyes the war was a holy one because a crusade against evil. Germany must be made to abandon for ever the unblest doctrine that Right was Might.

There is little more to tell, for the rest is, alas, already an old story among our young men, a story of hardships cheerfully borne and bravery modestly concealed. Though he was mentioned in despatches for gallantry and received the Military Cross, one could never get any account of the incident from him. There was still plenty of humour left in him; for instance, after he had been in hospital with jaundice, he wrote: "Trench warfare, after the Cambridge climate, is the most enervating thing I know." Yet there was always the impatience to do something. "England is a dreary place now, and I was really pleased when my sick leave ended. I spent two happy nights in Peterhouse, but Cambridge is no more than a melancholy haunt." It was again the old story—the overpowering emotion had made one whose natural bent was towards thought impatient to distinguish himself by action. The Cambridge and the England which he loved now stood between him and France. It was in France that he wished to be, and it is France which holds him now.

H. W. V. T.

The Essay *Palmerston and the Hungarian Revolution* is based, for the most part, on the Foreign Office records in Chancery Lane; and in every case where use has been made of these records, either in paraphrase or quotation, the source is indicated in footnotes. Not a few have appeared in print before, chiefly in Government publications. In such cases, reference has been made to the relevant Blue or White Books; but, where the printed copy differs materially from the MS original, I have used the latter, and as a rule noted the variation in my footnotes. Secondary authorities have been freely employed, but not without an attempt to appraise their worth as 'sources,' and never without sufficient indication of the use made of them either in the text or in the footnotes.

I have had no opportunity of working in the archives either at Vienna or Buda-Pest.

C. SPROXTON.

PALMERSTON
AND THE HUNGARIAN
REVOLUTION

" En fait d'histoire contemporaine il n'y a de
vrai que ce qu'on n'écrit point."
VAN DE WEYER.

PALMERSTON
AND THE HUNGARIAN
REVOLUTION

THE men who guided the larger destinies of Europe during the "storm-years" 1848 and 1849, were scarcely equal to the tasks which they were called upon, voluntarily or involuntarily, to accomplish; for these years do not merely bisect the century, they are its watershed. On the far side lie benevolent despotism and the state-system; on this side, democracy and nationalities. The period from the Congress of Vienna to the Civic Guard of Pius IX and the Hungarian Diet of 1847 is, in a very real sense, the fine flower of the eighteenth century. Territorial frontiers may have been shifted somewhat, old institutions rebaptised; but the spirit is the same: Joseph II would never have dared to do all that the Congresses did, and Guizot always speaks like a minister of Louis XV. The first French Revolution was only perceptible through the completeness of the reaction; so efficaciously had the body politic been purged that, outwardly at any rate, it appeared more immune from the revolutionary taint than it had in 1788. Then, with incredible swiftness, the house of reaction collapsed, and long flames of

rebellion shot across Europe from the Atlantic to
Bessarabia, from Posen to the shores of Sicily, almost
outrunning the telegraph which announced their
approach. And this, to use an outworn term, is the
"foundation" of modern Europe. The actors, with
a few exceptions (and these chiefly south of the Alps),
are not cast in a heroic mould: Viennese schoolboys,
preferring a *Katzenmusik* by night to carefully pruned
lectures on political science at more seasonable hours;
older, but scarcely more erudite, students, proclaim-
ing the divine right of a people whose history and
culture they had just manufactured; the degenerate
'48 breed of *sansculottes*, and Magyar *honveds*, magni-
fying some slight skirmish between outposts into a
Cannae or Waterloo. This is one of the reasons why
the European Revolution of 1848 will never be so
well known as the French Revolution of sixty years
earlier, although the judgment passed by the cautious
Springer upon the March-days of Vienna holds good
for the greater part of Europe, in spite of the fact
that he was speaking of Austria only:

We may take various views about the vitality of the
new Austria which they tried to set up on the ruins of
the old; but there can be no conflict of opinion that in the
March-days the old Austria fell completely, justly, and
for ever, and that all who have held power since 1848,
without distinction, take their stand upon the Revolution[1].

[1] "Ueber die Lebensfähigkeit des neuen Oesterreich, welches
auf den Trümmern des alten zu errichten versucht wurde,
kann man verschiedener Ansicht sein; dass aber in den
Märztagen *das alte Oesterreich vollständig, mit Recht und für
immer zu Grunde ging, alle Machthaber seit* 1848 *ohne Unter-*

During such momentous times, Palmerston, alone of those who were at the head of affairs, realised fully what the contemporary phenomena meant, whence they were derived, and to what profitable ends they might be utilised; he alone perceived that after the *Völkerfrühling* the political harvesting would not be as those that had gone before. This is not chauvinistic over-estimation; Palmerston is indeed the outstanding figure of 1848–9, a giant among his fellows, not because his proportions are in truth gigantic when measured by the tape of world-history, but because the Ficquelmonts and Drouyn de Lhuys are so very dwarfish. The space which divides him from Pitt, the disciple from the master, is the whole distance between the high-water mark of common-sense and the snow-line of genius. But the times were crying out for a little undiluted common-sense, which, as Lamartine discovered, may well be more fitted than genius to cope with revolution. Genius would never have made such gross miscalculations about the future as did Palmerston; but it would doubtless have dealt less vigorously with the present: short-sightedness is a virtue in some crises.

Palmerston, then, was not a great man; but he was the right man. Sir Stratford Canning, had he had any gifts of oratory, would have made a better Foreign Secretary; Schwarzenberg and Czar Nicholas were his equals as statesmen, while Lamartine and

schied auf die Revolution als ihre Basis fussen, darüber herrscht kein Zwiespalt der Meinungen." Springer, *Geschichte Oesterreichs seit dem Wiener Frieden,* vol. II. pp. 194–6, and footnote. (Leipzig, 1865.)

Mazzini were incomparably greater as men. And, if Palmerston judged the phenomena of his time accurately, and proceeded to take the steps he actually took, he was indebted to his country's geographical position no less than to his own innate commonsense. Not seldom has the Channel proved itself more potent than the personal element as a maker of history, and but for it many a Downing Street transgressor might have died repentant. Palmerston was on the right side of the Channel for the *rôle* he chose to play during the Revolution; and, standing outside the universal ferment, he got a better view of it. It is a comfortable pastime to read the *Mene Tekel* on a neighbour's wall, to "rain homilies" at Vienna and point the moral of governmental misdeeds in Athens, when one has nothing worse to face at home than potato famines in Ireland and Chartist signatories who have only a parchment existence. For his interference abroad Palmerston has been censured everywhere; at home, he frightened his colleagues and was found intolerable in exalted circles, while subsequent historians, such as Spencer Walpole and Sir Theodore Martin, cannot condemn too plainly his insolence and effrontery. Abroad, of course, he is still Lord *Feuerbrand*, and the European "umpire." In the English universities we are apologetic and indignant by turns, when speaking of the English Foreign Secretary who appointed himself tutor in *Weltpolitik* and lecturer in international ethics. The accusation is on the whole unjust, and the worst that can be said of Palmerston is that he was no diplomat in the nicer shades of the term. "In diplomacy," said de Tocqueville, "you must always write, even when you know nothing and wish to say nothing"; and he might have added that in nine cases out of ten you must take good care that you do not say anything. That was not Palmerston's way, and, except in rare moments of supremely correct behaviour, he usually did say something very unambiguously. Poor Lord Ponsonby, our ambassador at Vienna, the friend of Metternich and disciple of Talleyrand, told Lord John Russell that "he had received from Palmerston letters which are not to be submitted to by any man[1]"; and Palmerston was usually more brusque and less polite with foreign Courts than with his own servants, in spite of the watchful eye and ready pencil of Queen Victoria. To be impolite and insulting in diplomacy is a mistake; but it was Palmerston's only mistake. Impartial readers must admit that the kings and princes whom Palmerston called fools and knaves were not far from being such. A large section of the country—including the Queen and the Prince Consort—complained in 1849–50 that his *brusquerie* and habit of straight talking had left us without an ally in Europe. Palmerston replied that right and justice were stronger than troops of armed men[2], and his admirers may assert that the alliances were worthless, especially at the price at which they were to be purchased.

[1] Spencer Walpole, *Life of Lord John Russell*, vol. II. p. 48 footnote.

[2] Speech of July 21st, 1849, Debate on Russian Invasion of Hungary, House of Commons. Hansard, CVII. pp. 786–817.

Palmerston, it has been said, judged the movements of 1848 at their proper value. He did not fall into panic fear at what was happening, and many of his despatches are filled with the undisguised note of jubilation of a prophet justified in his prophesying at the last. He knew that the end of social order had not come in England, and, in spite of barricades and fugitive royalty, believed that the same was true of Europe. There was probably only one man, apart from himself, on whose judgment he placed any reliance, and that man strongly corroborated this belief. Before he took up his fifth residence in Constantinople in 1848, Sir Stratford Canning had been sent as itinerant ambassador to most of the Courts which lay between Ostend and the Golden Horn. He saw shivering burghers relieve the guard with white-gloved students in a deserted Berlin, and witnessed nocturnal disturbances at Vienna; and yet he wrote home his firm belief that Central Europe was sound at heart. What was true of Germany was true of the rest of Europe; and, if there was trouble ahead, it was the fault not of the peoples, but of the Courts. Napoleon had been finally overthrown, not by princes and statesmen, but by the citizen, the student and the artisan; not by diplomacy, but by the nascent force of nationality. And what had been the reward for the generation which lay between Waterloo and the Smoke-riots at Milan? There had been no reward: the novel sensation of a national self-consciousness, and all the hundred forms of a better life that it meant, had been protocolled out of existence at Troppau and Carlsbad. Not only had the doors of government been banged in the face of the citizen and artisan who had fought at Leipzig, but a despotism more brutal, and a delation more searching, than any that characterised the empire of Napoleon, intruded upon the innermost recesses of their private life. "Do you think," asked the Prince of Prussia, afterwards King and Kaiser Wilhelm, "that if the nations had known in 1813 that of all their struggling no reality, but only the remembrance, would remain—do you think anybody would have made sacrifices so great?" All the time social conditions were improving; inventors were never more active; banks were multiplying in great and small cities; commercial companies were being floated everywhere. The excluded classes were now something more than illiterate, half-starved peasants; they were travelled, prosperous, and had some sort of education. Whatever they might think at the Hofburg, humanity no longer began with barons. Such a state of things could not last for ever; apathy became discontent, discontent grew into disorder, and unless the Governments yielded, disorder would convert itself into revolution. In England the Government had yielded as early as 1832, and, in addition to the Reform Bill, there was a widely-read Press, and, for the artisans, some trades-union activity. Institutions which had been so beneficial in England would have similar salutary effects if applied to the European Continent—that is the whole statement of Palmerston's position, both before and after the outbreak.

He once told the Master of Trinity that no man ought to be doctored against his will: half his official life was spent in doctoring governments against their will. The student of the Foreign Office records for the later 'forties grows weary, in spite of Palmerston's crisp logic and sharply-etched metaphors, of the eternal prescription to the ailing but recalcitrant foreigner: "If you would but turn constitutional and copy our institutions, you might be as happy and prosperous, and sleep as soundly in your bed, as we in England." The advice was perfectly sound, and, had it been taken and acted upon in the spirit in which it was given, much disaster would certainly have been avoided. It is quite obvious from the *Memoirs* of Metternich that he, too, diagnosed the disease correctly and knew the remedy that should be applied. It would have been as well for his reputation had he never disclosed the fact. Thus Palmerston was no revolutionary, but honestly believed that political institutions which had proved themselves of sterling worth in the United Kingdom might with advantage be imported into Europe, and that, in any case, the old forms of government, as they had been fashioned under the auspices of the Holy Alliance, were no longer possible.

But however liberal and humane he might be, however frankly his sympathies might be enlisted on the side of oppressed nationalities, Palmerston was still Foreign Secretary, and in that capacity his chief duty was the maintenance of the Balance of Power. It might happen that humane considerations and the maintenance of the Balance of Power did not

always go hand in hand. In that case, the duty of a
British statesman clearly was to look to the latter
first. Charity and diplomacy, indeed, usually seemed
identical while Palmerston was at the Foreign Office;
and a despatch protesting against "Bomba's" latest
piece of cruelty, or the annexation of Cracow, or
arguing in favour of the asylum extended by the
Swiss to political refugees, was equally justified by
the doctrine of the Evangelists and by the doctrine
of the Balance of Power. To this rule there was one
great exception, and that exception was the revolution in Hungary: why it should have been an exception will be seen after a short résumé of Palmerston's
ideas of the Balance of Power has been attempted.

And here the fear of Russian preponderance is the
salient fact. Once that is comprehended, the maze is
threaded easily enough. Palmerston feared Russia,
and in doing so proved himself to be a man of his
generation. It is hard for us now to think ourselves
back into the forty years that separate the Moscow
campaign from the campaign in the Crimea, and to
realise the position which the Czar occupied during
that period in the eyes of the other European monarchs and statesmen. The rout of the *Grande Armée*,
and the entry of Alexander I into Paris remained
unforgotten—Russia had repaid her ancient debt to
Western civilization with interest. But it was not
merely the part played by Russia in the closing years
of the Napoleonic Wars that invested her with a
strength and grandeur which she did not in truth
possess. Even so recently as sixty years ago, Russia

was, comparatively speaking, unknown, and therefore held for magnificent. Her enormous mileage, her untold millions of fanatically loyal serfs, the unplumbed depths of the Slavonic character—these struck the imagination of the West, while the real weaknesses of the Muscovite polity remained undiscovered. There was something un-European about it all, something terrible; the saviour of the West might one day become its destroyer. This may seem exaggerated language as applied to a time within the memory of men still living, but it describes an actual state of affairs. De Tocqueville, the sanest of thinkers, firmly believed, on the eve of the Crimean War, that "our West is threatened, sooner or later, to fall under the yoke or at least under the direct and irresistible influence of the Czars"; and, Frenchman though he was, he thought that German unity should be fostered as a barrier between the threatening East and the threatened West[1]. In 1846, Hummelauer told Stockmar that "without Russia there would be no longer an Austrian State[2]." In England the same sentiment is displayed time after time in Parliamentary debates and in dozens of forgotten pamphlets; the strength and extent of the idea are perhaps best gauged from the writings of its chief opponent, Cobden. Already, in 1848, Panslavism—a Panslavism the headquarters of which were in St Petersburg—was a force in diplomacy,

[1] *Recollections of Alexis de Tocqueville*, edited by the Comte de Tocqueville, p. 350. (London, 1896.)

[2] Stockmar, *Memoirs*, vol. II. p. 360. The conversation took place after the Cracow affair.

and was to be the compensation to Russia for the
failure of the Holy Alliance. It will be seen that this
was at least one of the motives for the Russian intervention in Hungary in the spring months of 1849.
Side by side with the Panslav schemes in Russian
official circles went the hope of a Byzantine future;
in the West at any rate, the Czar was always supposed
to have one eye fixed on the dome of St Sofia and the
finest commercial and strategical position in the
world. There was always a Constantine in the family
to remind the Romanoffs of their ultimate destiny,
and, since there was a real religious justification for
the idea, it was popular with the masses. The imperial
epigram had long been public property: "The
Ottoman Empire is dead; we have only to arrange
for its funeral"—and the Czar meant to be sole heir.
The fear of Russian aggrandisement in the Balkans
underlay the whole of Stratford Canning's later work
at Constantinople, and there is no reason for believing
that the ambassador's anti-Russian counsels to
Palmerston and the Porte were the result of personal
pique, and not of genuine dread of the designs of the
Czar and his ministers. How real the danger was
may be seen from a despatch of Canning's sent home
in the early weeks of 1849, which encloses some
extracts from a book printed in Moscow, and intended
to be circulated in the European provinces of Turkey.
The chief extract is as follows: "Destroy quickly the
Empire of Hagar, infamous as it is and detestable to
Heaven, and give it to the orthodox Emperor; fortify
the true believers, raise up the Christian race, and do

not withdraw from us Thy great mercy[1]." The next day, in a private letter to Palmerston, Canning hints that the appearance of a fleet in the Archipelago would have a very good influence on the course of events in the Balkans. This was over half a year before the question of the refugees cropped up, and contemporaneous with the first incursion of the Russian troops into Transylvania, which involved a violation of Turkish territory. "If the Russians are only bullying," he writes, "a little more determination will keep them in order. If they have great schemes in view, it will be more necessary to check them. This is worthy of prompt and serious thought. The appearance of a combined squadron in these latitudes of force sufficient to go further if necessary, would probably set all to rights; and if one might hope that, spite of Cobden, the public would go with you against an exposed system of encroachment, hypocrisy, and despotic reaction, would not the establishments at home escape a severe trial, and the peace of Europe have a better chance of being secured....?

"In conversation with General Aupick," French minister at the Porte, "the other day, I found that he was entertaining the idea of a visit to the Dardanelles by a combined squadron, and I am inclined

[1] The Book was a book of psalms and prayers, and the extracts are given in a French translation: it begins, "*Au nom du Père, du Fils*, etc. *Par ordre du Très-Auguste et Très-Puissant Empereur Nicholas*, etc. *et avec la bénédiction du Saint Synode....Imprimé à Moscou au mois d'avril*, 1848." Canning to Palmerston, Feb. 4th, 1849.

to think that he has written home about it, though
not perhaps in an official form. Though not dissenting
from him, I was careful not to encourage him in any
exaggerated views, though, in truth, there is enough
in our present appearances here to warrant the
apprehension of circumstances requiring a strong
demonstration in favour of the Porte and our Oriental
policy[1]."

One of Canning's most cherished aims was to
ameliorate the condition of the Christian subjects of
the Sultan; he discovered that Russian intrigue was
striving to dissuade his friends in the Council of the
Porte from following his counsels in the matter,
because it was not to their interests that the Christians
of the Balkan Peninsula should be contented under
the rule of Islam. Equally clear and convincing is a
despatch written by the English chargé d'affaires
at St Petersburg after a conversation he had had
with the Russian chancellor, Count Nesselrode, on
the affairs of the Turkish Empire.

I may observe that what has struck me most in the
various conversations which I have had with Count
Nesselrode and other persons, with regard to this subject,

[1] Canning to Palmerston, Feb. 5th, 1849, Private Letter.
This was not the first time that Canning had hinted at the
appearance of an English fleet in the Archipelago. On
November 20th of the previous year he had written home that
Russia was so dictatorial and encroaching that it might be
advisable for the whole or part of our Mediterranean Fleet
(probably in conjunction with the French) to demonstrate in
the Levant and Archipelago. No English war-vessel had been
there for some time, and Russia had taken advantage of this
to assure the Sultan that the moral support of the Western
Powers was wanting. Nov. 20th, 1849.

is that they never discuss it without evincing unconsciously a latent conviction that the Turkish Empire
merely exists from the sufferance and magnanimity of
the Emperor; and that any suspicion therefore, which may
be thrown on His Imperial Majesty's policy towards the
Porte, is calling in question the self-denial, to which that
power is indebted for her existence; and that opposition,
on the part of a Foreign Government, to arrangements
which Russia may wish to concert with the Turkish
Authorities...is an absolute interference with the just
rights of His Imperial Majesty. As they are aware that
such pretensions will not be admitted by Europe, and
more particularly by the Government of Her Majesty,
they do not proclaim them; but, it appears to me, they
consider Her Majesty's Government, by the course which
they are pursuing in Turkey, to be raising questions on
technicalities and endeavouring to fence by legal sub-
tilties a falling Empire, which nothing could prevent the
Emperor, if he thought fit, from annexing to his dominions.

What is perhaps more surprising, I have found some of
my colleagues not altogether free from similar impressions...[1].

Palmerston was in no sense of the word a fanatical
hater of Russia. He had ample opportunity of
opening the old wound that was Poland, on any day
of the year, and would have been cheered to the
echo by almost any crowd in the British Isles. He
did not do so: "The Government will never do anything underhand or ungentlemanlike on those
matters," he said[2]. But he did fear Russia, and

[1] Buchanan to Palmerston, March 13th, 1849.
[2] Palmerston to Lord Bloomfield, April 11th, 1848, Bloomfield Papers.

nowhere so much as in the Near East. Consequently, he recognised it to be his duty to find a barrier to the encroachments of Russia westwards and southwards. In spite of her manifold transgressions against Albion and common-sense, in spite of her unfaithfulness and obstinacy, Austria was essentially and necessarily the ally of England against Russia; if Russian aggrandisement threatened the well-being of England a thousand miles away, how much more did it threaten that of Austria, which lay right athwart the path which the Czars had marked out for themselves! That which was dearest to the heart of the Russian statesmen, ran straight counter to the interests of Viennese diplomacy. If Constantinople became once again the capital of the Orthodox faith, Austria would be little more than a Russian *enclave*; if the Panslavic ideal were realised according to the wishes attributed to Nicholas and Count Nesselrode, Austria would lose some of her fairest provinces. The Austrian Government could not be ignorant of the fact that their Servian subjects were already coquetting with Russia[1], and a pro-Russian agitation would be much more dangerous to the integrity of

[1] "I received last night a confidential communication from Aali Pasha [Turkish minister for foreign affairs] to the following effect; the Servians of Austria, equally discontented with the Governments of Vienna and of Hungary, wish to separate themselves from the Empire, and either to incorporate their population with that of Turkish Servia under the authority of the Porte, or to throw themselves entirely into the arms of Russia." This was not a piece of diplomatic gossip. "The intelligence has been conveyed to the Porte as well by the Pasha of Belgrade as by the Servian Government." Canning to Palmerston, Nov. 3rd, 1848.

the Austrian Empire than the revolution in Hungary.

Not only was Austria the chief ally of England against Russia, she was the only one. Germany indeed has as good reasons as Austria to fear the expansion of Russia; but then Germany did not yet exist. Palmerston was sagacious enough to recognise that a United Germany must appear some day, and that when it did appear it ought to be the ally of England, since the two countries would have two common foes—Russia and France. But he was too good a Liberal to foster a Germany united on the commercial principles of the *Zollverein*, and told the Prince Consort that "any English Ministry would be thought to have much neglected its duty, and to have sacrificed the commercial interests of the country, if it did not make every proper effort to persuade the States of North Germany, who have not joined the *Zollverein*, to continue to refrain from doing so[1]." Meanwhile, Germany was not united, and if Frederick William did anything at all, it would most probably be what his august relative at St Petersburg told him to do. Nor could France be relied upon. Nominally, we were the friends of that country; but it was a singular friendship, the result of necessity rather than of choice, of outward circumstances rather than of an indwelling cordial understanding between the two countries. Their agents abroad appraised the "friendship" at headquarters at its proper worth, and carried on wretched

[1] Martin, *Life of the Prince Consort*, vol. II. pp. 447–8.

diplomatic squabbles in every quarter of the globe. And as the revolutionary movement spent its force, or was ruthlessly suppressed, the position of France was indeed a difficult one. After the Government had definitely broken with the "red fool-fury," after Cavaignac had restored order, and the reins of government had been handed to Louis Napoleon, the Administration was reduced to lead a "petty life, from day to day[1]"; it could not heartily cooperate with the restorers of order abroad, for that function belonged to Russia, and the Left at home was still powerful, and had to be placated. It could not join the innovators, for they were hopelessly incapable, and to support them abroad meant to fall beneath their blows at home. So the Government, if with an ill grace, must needs accept the "sterile goodwill of the English," and "remain haughty, while it ceased to be preponderant." In any case, the Prince-President had special reasons of his own for dealing tenderly with Russian susceptibilities, as will be seen later, and Palmerston was still smarting from the reverse he had suffered in the matter of the Spanish marriages, and the whole position of affairs in the Iberian Peninsula. With the conciliatory Aberdeen at the Foreign Office, a hearty cooperation of the two Governments would have been difficult enough to engineer; with "*ce terrible* Lord Palmerston"— openly accused by Queen Victoria herself of bringing about the fall of the July Monarchy—it was out of the question. The two countries did indeed "co-

[1] De Tocqueville, *op. cit.* pp. 340–1.

operate " in the question of the Hungarian and Polish refugees—but how unwillingly, and with what mutual distrust, is known to anyone who has gone through the relevant documents. Since the days of Mehemet Ali, English statesmen watched French activity in the Near East only less narrowly than they were wont to watch Russian movements in the same regions.

Austria, then, was the traditional and inevitable ally of England, and as such was regarded by Palmerston. The fact is patent in his despatches, in his parliamentary speeches, and in such records of his conversations at this date as are extant. Perhaps the most interesting passage of all is the account which the Hungarian Pulszky (of whose mission to England more hereafter) gives of an unofficial visit which he paid to Palmerston in the private room of the latter in Downing Street. Palmerston condemned the policy which Austria was pursuing with respect to Hungary, but remarked that the Austrian Empire was of such a nature

that, if it did not already exist, it would have to be invented; that it was an European necessity, and the natural ally of England in the East; he therefore counselled us to reconcile ourselves with Austria, because in the frame of the European State-system it would be impossible to replace Austria by small States[1].

[1] Pulszky, *Meine Zeit, mein Leben*, vol. II. p. 322 (4 vols. Pressburg and Leipzig, 1880–3). There is no reason to doubt the value of this portion of Pulszky's autobiography, especially since much that is contained in it is corroborated from other sources. The conversation reported above most likely took place in March, 1849, shortly after Pulszky had arrived in England.

Palmerston was here repeating verbatim, consciously or unconsciously, what Palacky had said in his famous refusal to join the Committee of Fifty. Equally explicit are his words in the House of Commons:

Austria is a most important element in the balance of European power. Austria stands in the centre of Europe, a barrier against encroachment on the one side, and against invasion on the other. The political independence and liberties of Europe are bound up, in my opinion, with the maintenance and integrity of Austria, as a great European Power; and therefore anything which tends by direct or even remote contingency, to weaken and to cripple Austria, but still more to reduce her from the position of a first-rate Power to that of a secondary State, must be a great calamity to Europe, and one which every Englishman ought to deprecate, and to try to prevent[1].

Palmerston, then, however unpalatable his advice to Vienna might be, did sincerely and for statesman-like reasons desire that the Austrian Empire should be maintained in all its strength, for purposes of the Balance of Power, which with him meant resistance to Russian aggression in South-eastern Europe. Whatever tended to weaken the might of Austria could hope for no help from him; this should have been obvious to anyone who was at all acquainted with his views on the European situation. His policy with regard to the Austrian possessions in North Italy is no exception; he believed, and was never

[1] Debate on Russian Intervention in Hungary, July 21st, 1849, Hansard, cvii.

tired of stating, both officially and otherwise, that the Italian possessions were a source of weakness and not of strength, to the Government at Vienna. They were on the wrong side of the Alps and too far from the centre of the Empire; they constantly required a large force to keep them in order. The Italians of Lombardy would never and could never become good Austrians. If all the energy and resources and attention of Austria were focused on the west, she would be the less able to fulfil her duties to the European polity in the east. Of course other considerations entered into these views. Historians, especially continental historians, believe that his jealousy of French influence led him to interfere so zealously as he did in favour of the Lombardo-Venetians, and doubtless the last thing that Palmerston would have desired was that the French should be preponderant in northern Italy. His sovereign believed that he was actuated by hatred of Austria pure and simple, and was cooperating with the French to drive the Austrians out of Italy. "The Queen," she wrote, "cannot conceal from him that she is ashamed of the policy which we are pursuing in this Italian controversy in abetting wrong[1]"; and she goes on to point out that if he took his stand on the treaties of 1815 in the Schleswig-Holstein affair, he ought for the sake of consistency to do the same in Italy. And on July 25th she wrote to Russell[2]:

[1] *Letters of Queen Victoria*, Ed. 1911, vol. II. p. 182. The Queen to Palmerston, July 1st, 1848.
[2] *Letters*, vol. II. pp. 186–7.

The Queen must tell Lord John what she has repeatedly told Lord Palmerston, but without apparent effect, that the establishment of an *entente cordiale with the French Republic*, for the purpose of driving the Austrians out of *their dominions* in Italy, would be a *disgrace* to this country. That the French would attach the greatest importance to it, and gain the greatest advantage by it, there can be no doubt of; but how will England appear before the world *at the moment* when she is struggling to maintain her supremacy in Ireland, and boasts to stand by treaties with regard to her European relations, having declined all this time to interfere in Italy, or to address one word of caution to the Sardinian Government on account of its attack on Austria[1], and having refused to mediate when called upon to do so by Austria, because the terms were not good enough for Sardinia, if she should ally herself with the arch-enemy of Austria to interfere *against her* at the moment when she has recovered in some degree her position in the Venetian territory?

On August 21st she wrote with a note of despair: "Lord Palmerston *will* have his Kingdom of Upper Italy under Charles Albert, to which every other consideration is to be sacrificed." On September 7th she characterised his idea of wresting the Italian Provinces from Austria by French arms as a

most iniquitous proceeding. It is another question whether it is good policy for Austria to try to retain Lombardy; but that is for her and not for us to decide. Many people might think that we should be happier without Ireland or Canada[2].

[1] This reproach was also hurled against Palmerston in Parliament; it was, however, not true: see the *Correspondence* (Bluebook) *on the Affairs of Italy*; and Helfert, *Geschichte der Oesterreichischen Revolution*, vol. I. p. 337.

[2] *Letters*, pp. 191, 194; and Friedjung, *Oesterreich von 1848 bis 1860*, vol. II. part I. p. 138. (Stuttgart and Berlin, 1912.)

Radetzky's army and the blunders of Charles Albert
upset Palmerston's plans, and he did not live to see
the last Austrian turn his back on the Po; but both
the Queen and Disraeli were mistaken when they
accused him of assuming "from the first squabble
between the monarch and some of his subjects...
that Austria was to be blotted out of the map of
nations." On the contrary, as has been stated, the
maintenance of the Austrian Empire as a power of
the first magnitude was one of the chief aims of his
statesmanship. He did sincerely long for Italian
"liberties," and was genuinely disgusted with the
administrative brutality of a foreign master in the
land where he had spent so many happy days in his
boyhood. But in his North-Italian policy he was
primarily thinking of Austria, whose chief work lay
along the Russian frontier, and for whom Lombardo-
Venetia was in truth not the "shield of Ajax," but
the "heel of Achilles"; if he was cruel to the Austria
of 1848, it was that he might be kind to the Austria
of the future. That matters were not regarded in the
same light at Vienna, is neither an occasion of offence
nor of surprise[1]; but Teutonic sympathies and regard

Queen Victoria's Letters and Memoranda on Palmerston's
policy in the late 'forties, are perhaps the most remarkable
series of royal documents in modern history.

[1] In point of fact, there was a deeply-rooted feeling in
Austria and Germany, in 1848-9, that the North-Italian
possessions (or at any rate Lombardy) should be completely
renounced; see the quotations from contemporary newspapers, e.g. the *Augsburger Allgemeine Zeitung*, given in
Springer, *op. cit.* vol. II. pp. 242-3. And in May, 1848, before
Radetzky's victories of course, Hummelauer told Stockmar
that "Austria believes she has to found a new Empire, which
is, for the first time, to render its old name illustrious; and she

for the inviolable settlement of 1815—which had
been violated more than once by every Government
in Europe—should not have blinded the Court of
St James'.

But it is in his attitude to the Hungarian Revolution that Palmerston's policy with respect to Austria
is best seen. With the internal history of that movement, and its origins, we are not here concerned.
But, if successful, it would have made Hungary
de facto, what the Magyar patriots claimed that it
always had been *de jure*, completely independent of
the Austrian Hereditary Provinces, and united to
them by the barest of personal unions. At first, it
seemed as if this was actually to happen, for the
Opposition, supreme alike in the Diet at Pressburg,
and in the country, carried everything before them,
and, on April 10th, the Emperor-King Ferdinand
gave his approval to the Bills of the preceding
session, which freed the country from the rule of the
Viennese bureaucracy, and secured Hungary to the
Hungarians. A Hungarian cabinet was set up, with
Count Louis Batthyányi as minister-president, which
was responsible to the Emperor alone; and, for the
time being, the Archduke Stephen, Palatine of the
land, was invested with full regal powers. That the
whole of the country, even of the strictly Magyar
population, was behind the movement, cannot be
asserted. The greater nobles were opposed to it, if

will therefore make Hungary the nucleus of a new State, and,
if necessary, even place the capital there." Stockmar, *Memoirs*,
vol. II. p. 355.

for no other reason, because it meant the loss of their feudal rights and privileges—especially their century-old, though in part (1832) repealed, immunity from taxation—and not more than a mere handful, of whom the chief were the Batthyányis, Count Ladislaus Teleki, and Count Julius Andrássy, joined it at any time. The most renowned of all the nobles, Count Stephen Széchenyi, though strenuously in favour of economic and social progress, was opposed from the very first to that complete separation from the Hereditary Provinces which Kossuth and his followers had in view. And Francis Deák, a greater statesman and profounder thinker than Széchenyi, passed the severest condemnation which it is possible for a man to pass on the April Laws: "You cannot talk reason with a drunken man, and at present the Diet is drunk." Nor was it only the greater nobles that held aloof from the movement: a large proportion of the educated classes, and many members of the liberal professions, were opposed to it, and perhaps the majority of the really rich burgher population. But in the mid-months of 1848 it really looked as if Kossuth's tongue would undo the history of more than three hundred years, and destroy the Balance of Power in Europe. Frankfort was delighted, for a united Germany and an independent Hungary seemed natural allies. The Magyars perceived that a strong and united Germany would prevent a Slav preponderance in the Austrian Empire, while the Germans saw that the Government at Vienna would either oppose the unity of the

Fatherland, or would at any rate insist on the hegemony therein. But the fangs of Austria were drawn, if Hungary ceased to be merely a part and parcel of it. "In Hungary," said Bunsen, "they are fighting a battle in which the victory of the Germans may easily lead to the slavery of Germany—not in a distant future, but for the present generation[1]." The democrats at Vienna fraternised with their brothers beyond the Leitha, recognising the common cause of the new-born peoples against a dying despotism and an out-worn bureaucracy; and, although the Wessenberg-Bach Ministry were in their hearts of course opposed to the Hungarian Revolution, they dared not say so openly. But the unbroken course of Magyar success was not to continue for long, and there were rocks in plenty ahead. After all, the true-born Magyars were but an island in an ocean of alien stems; to these stems—various branches of the great Slav family—Kossuth and his friends showed scant consideration in the moment of triumph. On whatever grounds the Magyars might justify their recent proceedings against the German monopoly of government in Hungary— nationality, numbers or history—the surrounding races had equally good grounds, or could plausibly claim that they had, for objecting to a Magyar hegemony in their own regions. But the majority of the Diet now at Pest, the capital, was distinguished neither by consistency nor by compassionateness.

Although the unprejudiced student must decide,

[1] Bunsen, *Tagebücher*, vol. III. p. 1.

in nine cases out of ten, for the Magyars as against
the Government at Vienna, he will recognise that
the ultimate failure of the former was largely due to
the arrogance and injustice they had displayed, in
the first instance, towards the neighbouring races.
Strife was perhaps in any case inevitable, in a
country which was ethnologically a veritable mosaic,
at a time when national *Gleichberechtigung* was the
order of the day. Long before 1848 had run its
course, anti-Magyar movements had appeared everywhere except in the plains watered by the Theiss
and the Upper Danube, where the population was
homogeneous: in Galicia towards the north, among
the Roumanians and German colonists of Transylvania in the east, and among the Croats and Serbs of
Croatia, the Banat and the Military Frontier. These
movements were not at first dynastic or Austrian,
and threatened the integrity of the Empire every
whit as much as did the Magyar. It was due to the
sentiments and genius of one man that the chief of
them, the Croatian, became of almost decisive moment in the restoration of the Emperor's authority.
From the first, Jellačič, Ban of Croatia, had been
recognised at Pest as an enemy to be brought over
or annihilated; and, on June 10th, 1848, an imperial
manifesto degraded him from his offices and branded
him as a traitor. But the Court was merely biding
its time, and waiting for favourable news from Italy.

In the first week of August, Radetzky entered Milan
in triumph, and within a month another rescript
was published by Ferdinand—secure behind the

guns of Olmütz—annulling the declaration of June
10th, and restoring Jellačič to all his former honours.
That was on September 4th; exactly a week later,
the Ban crossed the Drave into Hungary, at the head
of an army. The war in Hungary had begun. Already
in August the Palatine's vice-regal powers had been
withdrawn, and on September 25th he resigned. On
October 3rd, after Jellačič had been compelled to
withdraw as a result of the engagement at Velenze,
an imperial manifesto was published which dissolved
the Hungarian Diet, and declared its late resolutions
null; a state of siege was proclaimed over the whole
land, and Jellačič was appointed vicegerent of the
King (*Stellvertreter des Königs*) and Commander-in-
Chief of the troops in Hungary. So far no soldiers
had been actually sent from Vienna to take the
field against the Hungarians, but on October 5th
the Government sent off an Italian battalion; next
day an attempt was made to despatch Austrian
troops, and this was the immediate cause of the
third and last Viennese Revolution of 1848. Had the
Hungarians acted vigorously, they might have
dictated their own terms to the Court party in the
capital of the Empire; but they were strangely
dilatory, and had scruples about "invading" the
Hereditary Provinces until they should have received
a definite invitation from the Viennese democrats.
When they finally did move forward, it was too late:
for Windischgrätz, the conqueror of Prague, had
already united with Jellačič, and the conduct of the
Hungarian leaders was not of the sort that wins

battles. They met with a reverse from the Imperialists at Schwechat on October 30th, and fled back across the frontier. On the next day Vienna fell. After the battle of Schwechat, the Hungarians had nothing to hope for from the Viennese, large numbers of whom they had already alienated by their outspoken condemnation of the continuous disturbances in the city, and of the month-long anarchy there. They had, also, wounded the national pride of the Austrians by their reluctance to furnish Magyar troops for the Italian war, and had made enemies of the prosperous classes by their refusal to take over part of the Austrian national debt. The war would now be fought on their own soil and would be a war to the finish. The complete triumph of the anti-Magyar Court party was marked by the accession on December 2nd of the eighteen-year-old Francis Joseph; his uncle the Emperor Ferdinand had been induced to resign the Crown, and his father the Archduke Francis Charles to waive his right. The Hungarian Diet, which had taken no notice of the rescript of October 3rd, with every legal right in the world declared the accession of the new King unconstitutional, and still transacted business in the name of King Ferdinand. Meanwhile, Windischgrätz, with Fabian slowness although not with Fabian wisdom, had been preparing for the invasion of Hungary, and on January 5th, 1849, the Austrians entered Buda-Pest. Kossuth and the Government had already fled to Debreczin on the Theiss. During the early weeks of the new year nothing of moment was decided between the antagonists; and, except in the official bulletins of each side, no great battles were fought and no heavy losses sustained. But, while Windischgrätz was cumbrously arranging the organisation of the occupied but unconquered regions, the Magyars were preparing for a war *à outrance*. The battle of Kapolna marks the turning-point; although, tactically, the victory rested with the Austrians and they became lords of Hungary up to the Theiss, from the strategic point of view the tide had already set in for the Hungarians (February 26–27). As the winter passed away, the Hungarian recruits proved less unequal to the Imperialists in discipline and experience, and their numbers were being daily increased by the energetic action of the Committee of Defence at Debreczin. In the last days of March, Arthur Görgei was named Commander-in-Chief; in less than a month he had won three considerable battles, and on April 22nd he entered the fortress of Komorn, the key of the west, in triumph. Bem in Transylvania, and Perczel in the south, were equally successful. The Magyars were masters of their country once again, with the exception of the three strong places Arad, Buda and Temesvar; and Windischgrätz was removed from his command. All the world knew that, when a favourable opportunity should arise, the Austrian Government (where Schwarzenberg was now at the head of affairs) intended to dissolve the Diet at Kremsier, and to impose a centralising constitution on the whole Empire, including Hungary. This moment was considered to have arrived after

the victory at Kapolna, and on March 4th the famous
Constitution octroyée was published. This instrument
virtually annihilated the Hungarian Constitution, and
gave to the Magyars a watchword which would have
been intelligible to the whole of Europe. Nor was it
more acceptable to the other races of the Empire
whom it so ruthlessly disillusioned: the Slavs of the
south read in it the negation of all their hopes, and
from that moment hated the dynasty for whom they
had just been shedding their blood. A little clever
diplomacy at Debreczin might have worked wonders
amongst the late antagonists of the Magyars. But
Kossuth's was a bolder game, and he answered the
octroyée Constitution with the Declaration of Independence of April 14th, which proclaimed the depo-
sition for ever of the perjured Habsburgs from the
throne of St Stephen; until the form of government
should be finally decided, Kossuth was asked, and of
course consented, to carry on the executive. This is no
occasion for passing judgment on the Declaration of
Independence; ethically, there is much to be said in
its favour. But it certainly did not square with the
conscience of the majority of Hungarians, whose
passion for legality was incorrigible, and it was
notoriously unpopular in the camps. Under whatever
banner they might fight henceforth, their battlecry
could no longer be a protest of legality against
illegality: compared with the Declaration of Independence, the Constitution of March 4th was innocence
itself. Meanwhile, with Görgei at Komorn, the events
of 1848 were repeating themselves. There was no

longer any formidable Austrian army save that of
Radetzky in Italy, and a short vigorous march
would have seen the Hungarians masters of Vienna
in the opening days of May. Once again, the opportunity was neglected—Görgei's strategical justification of his conduct is anything but convincing—and,
after some days spent at Komorn, the Hungarian
commander turned eastwards, resolved to lay siege
to the fortress of Buda at his leisure. Henceforth,
the cause of the Magyars was hopeless. On May 1st,
the *Wiener Zeitung* announced that the Austrian
Government had been induced to solicit the armed
assistance of the Emperor of Russia; and, on May
11th, the *Journal de St Pétersbourg* printed the
Czar's manifesto in reply: "We shall not refuse."
For a time, the Hungarian papers tried to hide the
fact from the people, and spoke of differences between
Russia and Austria, which must finally lead to a war
between the two Powers; but, on May 17th, even the
Közlöny was constrained to admit officially the reality
of the intervention. After that, the restoration of
"order" could only be a question of weeks. Attacked
from every point of the compass, and weakened by
fatal internal dissensions, the various Hungarian
corps fought with a bravery that did not belie their
reputation of a thousand years; and Görgei did not
finally lay down his arms at the feet of the Russian
commander until August 13th. Whatever his motives
were—and the charge of treason is certainly not
proved—the surrender at Világos saved much boot-
less suffering and futile bloodshed; but it is equally

indisputable that Görgei might have been—and, under any Government more settled than that of Hungary in 1848-9, doubtless would have been—court-martialled for several of his actions during the earlier course of the struggle. Nothing remained now but for the imperial victors to punish the crimes of a year and a half of revolution. On October 5th General Klapka, the last warrior of the struggle for independence, surrendered the fortress of Komorn; and on the following day the bloody assizes were opened at Arad[1].

When, in the spring months of 1848, the establishment of an independent Hungarian Ministry received the imperial sanction, the condition of Europe beyond the frontiers of the Dual Monarchy was very favourable to the Magyar claims. It has been already mentioned that the Assembly at Frankfort was strongly in favour of these claims, and indeed, on July 22nd, declared unanimously for an alliance with the Government at Pest. Already in May, Ladislaus Szalay and Dionys Pazmandy (who later

[1] The best and most recent account of the Hungarian movement is that given by Friedjung, *Oesterreich von 1848 bis 1860*, vol. I., 2nd ed., 1908. Springer, whose book was published in 1865, is more detailed; he had no access to the vast mass of material, public and private, which Friedjung was able to draw upon; but his general conclusions will probably never be assailed. Helfert's work, *Geschichte Oesterreichs vom Ausgang des Wiener Aufstandes* (4 vols., Prague, 1869-86) is, also, of the greatest value. The libraryful of contemporary histories, memoirs, *Enthüllungen*, etc. is of no value to anyone save the historian of passion and error. The *Histoire Politique de la Révolution*, by Irányi and Chassin (2 vols., Paris, 1859), though written by a Parisian democrat and a Magyar revolu-

became President of the Hungarian Chamber), had been named Hungarian plenipotentiaries to the Central Power; and, when they passed through Vienna on their way to Frankfort, Pillersdorf, President of the Austrian Cabinet, told the Minister for Hungary in Vienna, Prince Esterházy, that he completely approved of the full powers and instructions which had been given to them, and had himself nothing to add. These instructions could not be very acceptable to the Austrians, for they frankly looked forward to a state of affairs when the Hereditary Provinces should be a mere fraction of that greater Germany which was to be the close ally of a powerful and independent Hungary. As to this there were no delusions at Vienna; and that the Ministry left open for future use the back door of chicanery, was shown by its referring to Szalay and Pazmandy, not as plenipotentiaries of the Hungarian Government, but as delegates (*Abgeordnete des ungarischen Reichstages*); inasmuch as their credentials were not signed by the Emperor-King, the issue of a formal "*lettre de créance*" could always be denied, if necessary[1]. The whole wretched ambiguity was turned

tionary, contains much that is indispensable. Most of the documents that matter are to be found in Adlerstein, *Archiv des ungarischen Ministeriums und Landesvertheidigungsausschusses* (3 vols., Altenburg, 1851). The Dahlmann-Waitz Bibliography is very poor for this period.

[1] See Springer, vol. II. p. 497, and Alter, *Die auswärtige Politik der ungarischen Revolution*, 1848–49, pp. 27–32 (Berlin, 1912, *unter Benutzung neuer Quellen*); also, W. H. Stiles, *Austria in* 1848–49 (2 vols., Washington, 1852) and Schlesinger, *Aus Ungarn* (Vienna, 1850). Alter's account of the Frankfort

to account, long afterwards, in the trial of Count
Louis Batthyányi. At Frankfort, Schmerling, in his
passion for correctness, refused to overlook the
diplomatic flaw; and since Szalay could not obtain a
recognition of his ambassadorial character, he left
the town in the early days of October, to coquet with
the democrats at Baden.

But it was from the two free and constitutional
Powers of the west that Kossuth hoped for the
greatest things. England had always been the
declared enemy of reaction, and the avowed friend
of struggling nationalities; while Lamartine had
recently declared that France could never allow the
treaties of 1815 to be used as a pretext for withholding
from the people their inherent rights. Almost
without exception, the extant memoirs and pamphlets
written by contemporary English and French travellers in Hungary are violently anti-Austrian, and at
Pest the English and French residents publicly
congratulated the new-born nation. When, on
March 15th, three-hundred Hungarians repaired to
the Hôtel de Ville in Paris and presented an address
to the Provisional Government of the French Republic, Lamartine responded: "*La Hongrie compte en
France autant d'amis qu'il y a de citoyens français!* [1]"
Moreover, Kossuth honestly believed that France
and England must perceive that a free and powerful

mission is taken from these latter two works. Stiles was
U.S.A. agent at Vienna at the time, and his relations with the
Party of Independence in Hungary were especially cordial.

[1] Irányi and Chassin, vol. I. p. 196.

Hungary, whose sole connexion with Austria proper was the slender *nexus* of a personal union, was the best safeguard of the Balance of Power in the East, although he never seems to have laid down with logical precision why the Balance of Power should be specially safeguarded by such a circumstance. In his more oratorical moments, he was even wont to assert that the two countries were under a moral obligation to defend the constitutional conquests of April, 1848. Kossuth never committed a graver error of judgment, for it is perfectly clear that neither England nor France was prepared to equip a single battalion or furnish a single ship to fight for the cause of Hungarian independence. Kossuth was not alone in his mistake, and the traveller in Hungary today is constantly asked the secret reason why England did not intervene in favour of the patriots of 1848–9, when Palmerston was so obviously in favour of such intervention; while, at the time, hundreds of English Radicals were quite certain that the real wishes of the Foreign Office were frustrated by a German camarilla at St James'. The whole matter may be summed up in a few words. Palmerston believed that the independence of Hungary was quite incompatible with the one essential task which the Dual Monarchy had to perform—the turning-back of the tide of Russian aggrandisement westwards and southwards. Kossuth beheld the English statesman's policy in Italy, believed that it was dictated by purely anti-Austrian sentiments, and naturally deduced therefrom the further belief, that Palmerston

could not choose but look favourably upon the
Hungarian movement. This was a fundamental
mistake; for Palmerston was not the murderer, but
the surgeon, of Austria. As he saw things, the cession
of the Italian Provinces was the amputation calculated to fit Austria for her real life-work; to make
Hungary independent was to cripple the Monarchy
in its most vital organ. To such maiming he would
be no party; and he was perfectly candid in his
views from the very first. If the Hungarians were
deceived, it was not through anything that had
reached them from the English Foreign Office. Not
once had the Queen to chide him for his pro-Magyar
sympathies, before it was quite clear that the Magyar
cause was hopeless. After the Russian intervention
in Hungary, he forfeited much of his popularity in
England, and was accused by many of his own party
of hobnobbing with the butchers of St Petersburg
and Vienna, simply and solely because he was
determined that Austria should be strong, and able
to fulfil her duty to the West. After Világos, he
made an attempt to save the Hungarians, but not
Hungary. What follows is merely an amplifica-
tion of, and comment upon, this judgment of his
conduct.

The Hungarians did not, indeed, fail, through lack
of assiduity or perseverance, to obtain help from
either England or France; but from the Government
of neither country were they able to obtain a recognition of their independence and, consequently, the
establishment of regular diplomatic intercourse.

According to Alter, in May, 1848, a Note was despatched to the French Foreign Office, and a similar Note was sent off, about the same time, to Palmerston. These Notes requested the consent of the two Governments to the appointment of Hungarian representatives at Paris and London, and asked that French and English diplomatic agents should be sent to Hungary. Both Foreign Secretaries, Bastide for France and Palmerston for England, responded in a manner which was scarcely calculated to raise enthusiasm at Buda-Pest. The French Government refused to make any binding declaration, and for the present reserved its final decision; but a French agent without diplomatic character was sent to Hungary to inform the Government of the true state of affairs. Palmerston's answer did not differ essentially from that of Bastide: the receipt of the Hungarian Note was formally acknowledged; but any sort of decision was reserved until the Government was aware of completed facts of real political worth. Until then, the English Government did not think that diplomatic correspondence was a necessity[1].

[1] Alter, pp. 48–52. Alter gives no date for the English Note and Palmerston's answer, and his references are merely "Batthyanyi and Palmerston, London, Archiv des Foreign Office," and "Palmerston and Batthyányi, A. d. F. O." I have not seen the documents in the Foreign Office records in Chancery Lane, and they are not to be found in the Bluebook, *Correspondence relative to the Affairs of Hungary, 1847–9, presented to both Houses of Parliament by Command of Her Majesty*, August 15th, 1850. But the Note was doubtless sent; see Kossuth's speech of July 11th, 1848, and the letter of the English Agent, Blackwell, to Palmerston, Oct. 5th, 1849. The letter says that in April, 1838, the Hungarians requested

How bitter Kossuth's disappointment was, is seen in
the speech on the defences of the country, which he
delivered in the Lower House of the Diet on July 11th,
1848. The Hungarian Cabinet, he declared, immediately after its accession to power, had placed itself
in communication with the English Government,
and pointed out to the latter that there was no truth
in the accusations which so many people were trying
to spread abroad[1]; the Hungarians had not wrested
their rights and freedoms from their King by virtue
of an insurrection, but stood on common ground with
him. They had also pointed out how the interests
of the two countries in the regions of the Lower

the English Government to establish a Consulship at Pest. It
may here be stated that the whole of Alter's work at the English and Parisian Archives was done for him by another hand.
The references to our Foreign Office records throughout his
book are almost invariably wrong, except in the case of those
despatches which were printed in the Bluebook. A portion
of his work, for instance, is taken up with the narration of the
plans of alliance between the Hungarians and Sardinians, and
his chief authorities are the despatches of a certain "Sir
Hudson," whom he states to have been English Minister at
Turin, to Palmerston. Abercromby was, of course, our Minister
at Turin in 1848–9, and during his absence Bingham was Chargé
d'Affaires. Nor was there any English agent, diplomatic or
consular, of that name in Italy at the time. Moreover, I have
gone carefully through the Sardinian volumes at the Record
Office, and can find nothing which in the least corresponds to
the despatches so freely "used" by Alter. His orthography
of English names is not impeccable, either, e.g. Ponsonby is
always referred to as "Posonby." It is only fair to add that,
except for mere errors of pagination, he is quite trustworthy
when using French and German published works.

[1] This may well have been a reference to the English Ambassador at Vienna, Lord Ponsonby, whose anti-Magyar sentiments
Kossuth and his friends had ample opportunities of knowing.

Danube were identical. They had received a reply on the part of the English Government, such as they might have expected from the liberal views, such also as they might have expected from the egoistically matter-of-fact policy, of that nation. In the meantime, they might be assured that England would only assist them in so far as she found it consistent with her own interests. Concerning France, the orator was yet more outspoken. The French were indeed the heralds of freedom in the old world, but it would never do to make the existence of the Hungarian nation dependent on the protection and alliance of France. Had not France at that very moment lived through another Eighteenth of Brumaire? She stood on the threshold of a dictatorship; the world might see a second Washington appear, but it might also see a second Napoleon. One thing at least could be learnt from the example of France: not every revolution was in the interests of freedom, and a nation was never so near the yoke of slavery as when, in searching after freedom, it found license. In the streets of Paris the blood of twenty thousand citizens had been shed by the hands of their fellows. For the rest, whether Cavaignac proved himself Washington or Napoleon, one thing was certain—France was far away. Poland, too, had relied on French sympathies. The sympathy had indeed existed; but Poland was no more[1].

[1] Adlerstein, *op. cit.* vol. ii. pp. 58–9. Irányi and Chassin, *op. cit.* vol. ii. pp. 14–17. *Memoir of Louis Kossuth*, by E. O. S. (London, 1854), p. 343.

The Hungarians had far more reason for bitterness against the French Government than against the English; but they ought not to have been victims of any delusions about the matter, since it was patent to all Europe that a reaction had set in at Paris after the June disturbances had been quelled. Cavaignac and Bastide could not afford to play with schemes of a Franco-Hungarian alliance, for their chief concern was to show the Czar that he had nothing to fear from the French Republic, and to this end it was necessary to hold aloof from all Governments infected with the revolutionary taint, into which category the Government at Pest certainly fell. The Russian Chancellor Nesselrode was never tired of emphasising to General Leflô, the French ambassador in St Petersburg, the solidarity of Austria and Russia in European affairs. Towards the revolutionary allies of the Pest Government, also, the Frankfort Assembly and the promoters of a united Italy, the French Government in the autumn of 1848 showed itself very reserved, for reasons not solely connected with the desire to do that which was pleasing to the eyes of Nicholas and his Minister Nesselrode.

In September Count Ladislaus Teleki was chosen by the Diet Hungarian Minister in Paris, perhaps the chief motive of his appointment being the wish of his numerous friends to free him from the influence of ultra-radical comrades in Pest[1]. His chief char-

---

[1] Springer, vol. II. p. 600, footnote: quoted by Alter, p. 82. Irányi and Chassin assert that Teleki arrived in Paris at the beginning of September, vol. II. p. 463.

acteristic was an unlimited capacity for committing his Government, without any sort of authorisation, to his own hare-brained schemes. He was received only in a private capacity by Bastide and Cavaignac. A fair sample of his judgment may be found in his belief, down to the very eve of the presidential elections, that Ledru-Rollin would be the fortunate candidate: then, he said, Hungary would be sure of support! After the election of Louis Napoleon, Teleki was no longer received by any French Minister, and he had to content himself with the friendship of the extreme Left and a few Legitimists. He and an able staff were very active in the French Press, and he managed to trouble the Prince-President with considerable persistency by way of the letter-box. As the clouds gathered more thickly over Hungary, and communication with the outside world became more difficult, the whole management of foreign affairs gradually fell into Teleki's hands. Towards the close of the year, when Windischgrätz was preparing to march on Pest, Teleki received orders from the Government to send Szalay, the quondam Minister at Frankfort, to England. On December 11th, the latter sent his credentials through the post to Palmerston. In his accompanying letter, Szalay reminded Palmerston that it was an Englishman who at the beginning of the eighteenth century had mediated between Hungary and Austria during the insurrection of Rákóczy. "This fact alone conclusively proves," he wrote, "that the relations of the Hungarian Crown to Austria have always been

considered as being within the domain of international law, as a portion of those questions which
have to be decided by the concurrence of the Great
Powers." The credentials themselves offered a
tempting bait to the Foreign Secretary of a nation of
shop-keepers, and are worthy of quotation in their
entirety.

Budapest,
November 12th, '48.

Sir,

Considering that Hungary, by its geographical
position, by the amount and richness of its natural pro-
ductions, is able to offer immense advantages to English
industry, which has been so prodigiously developed, and
that the establishment of commercial relations between
the two countries might be of great importance to Great
Britain herself, I have to request you, in the name of
the Hungarian Government, to call the attention of the
Cabinet of her Britannic Majesty to our country, and to
offer to that Cabinet all information necessary to explain
our actual position.

You will in the first place show, that if Hungary were
to revert to the bonds which united her to Austria before
the events of March, English industry and commerce
would for ever remain excluded from the markets of
Hungary, which Austria would continue to monopolise.

You will endeavour to give to the Government of Her
Britannic Majesty a just notion of the course of events of
which our country has become the theatre. You will, for
this purpose, show how desirous we were to make to the
Austrian Dynasty all concessions in any way compatible
with the welfare of our country, even to the prejudice of
our good right, founded on our laws, which guarantee
the independence of Hungary, and, although driven to

extremities, we have yet taken special care not to quit
the legal ground laid down by so many oaths of
Sovereigns.

You will show all the atrocities to which we have had to
submit on the part of the Austrian Court, notwithstanding
our perfectly loyal conduct.

Should, however, the great nation, alive to its own
interests, show a disposition to protect a cause so just as
ours, you are authorised to open preliminary negotiations
with the British Government in the name of the Government of Hungary. Such negotiations must, however, not
be definitively concluded, except by a treaty to be made
by an Envoy of the British Government to Hungary.

As regards the statistical basis of such negotiations, you
have only to refer to the commercial tables officially
published by the Austrian Statistical Department; these
tables will dissolve even the shadow of a doubt of
exaggeration on our part.

Assure the Cabinet of Her Majesty of our most perfect
consideration, and employ in the execution of your
commission all that zeal which we are accustomed to
find in you.

The President of the National Committee of Defence.
(Signed) LOUIS KOSSUTH[1].

On December 13th Lord Eddisbury, the Under-
Secretary for Foreign Affairs, replied in a manner so
correct and formal that neither Queen Victoria nor
Schwarzenberg could have desired to add or erase a
single word.

Sir,

I am directed by Viscount Palmerston to acknowledge the receipt of your letter of the 11th inst., and in

[1] *Correspondence relative to the Affairs of Hungary*, No. 78,
Szalay to Palmerston, Dec. 11th, 1848, and Enclosure.

reply I am to say that Viscount Palmerston is sorry he cannot receive you. The British Government has no knowledge of Hungary except as one of the component parts of the Austrian Empire; and any communication which you have to make to Her Majesty's Government in regard to the commercial intercourse between Great Britain and Hungary should therefore be made through Baron Koller, the Representative of the Emperor of Austria at this Court[1].

Szalay in his answer refuted the charge that Hungary was one of the "component parts of the Austrian Empire," with a quotation from the famous Tenth Article of the Diet of 1790–1: *De independentia Regni Hungariae*. He likewise pointed out that it was hardly to be expected that the envoy of the Hungarian Government should select one "whose functions emanate from a Ministry at open war with Hungary," as the channel for his communications with the British Government.

But there are countries which may not be conquered; Hungary is of that number. And the Government of that country flattered itself that Great Britain would listen to the information offered as to the actual state of the countries appertaining to the Hungarian Crown; that Great Britain, seeing that among all territories called Austrian, it was Hungary alone that remained excluded from the ultra-Democratic tempest, and looking to the immense resources of the kingdom, would draw the inference that Hungary is qualified to form the centre round which further provinces may group, and will group, themselves, capable of forming a sufficiently great and

[1] *Correspondence*, No. 79, Eddisbury to Szalay, Dec. 13th, 1848.

extended political organisation to afford guarantees for order and for wise and beneficent liberty; the Government of Hungary was happy to believe that Great Britain, in the interest of Europe, and her own interest, would hold out a ready and firm hand to assist Hungary in the accomplishment of this work.

It appears to me, My Lord, that the question of my official reception might be adjourned until I should have furnished you with such information on the actual state of Hungary as might guide the Government of Her Britannic Majesty in any further steps which they might take as regards Hungary. It is in this hope that I have the honour to notify Your Lordship that I shall stay some time longer in London[1].

Four days later came the more than laconic response:

In reply to your letter of the 15th instant, I am directed by Viscount Palmerston to say that Her Majesty's Government can take no cognizance of those internal questions between Hungary and the Austrian dominions to which your letter refers; but that the British Government has no diplomatic relations with Hungary except as a component part of the Austrian Empire, and can receive communications respecting Hungary only through the diplomatic organ of the Emperor of Austria at this Court[2].

After this latter reply, even Szalay perceived the hopelessness of the mission, and returned to Switzerland and his Baden revolutionaries. Perhaps, during

[1] *Correspondence*, No. 80, Szalay to Palmerston, Dec. 15th, 1848.
[2] *Correspondence*, No. 82, Eddisbury to Szalay, Dec. 19th, 1848.

his stay in London, he may have written home what must have been manifest to the most complete stranger in the metropolis: that the English were for the most part entirely indifferent to the fortune of arms on the Danube and Theiss, and at best luke-warm for the Hungarian cause. During 1848, there was a tremendous amount of enthusiasm in the country for the rebellious Lombardo-Venetians, when one considers how little interest either inside or outside Parliament is usually demonstrated in this insular kingdom for foreign affairs. But there was none for the Hungarians; whether we read the Foreign Office records for 1848, or the leading newspapers, the space devoted to their affairs is surprisingly small. Egoism—as Kossuth had hinted on July 11th —doubtless had something to do with this; whatever the Magyars might believe, the Russell administra-tion and the vast mass of the electorate did not hold that the Hungarian cause and European liberty stood and fell together. Much less was it an article of faith in London that English interests proper would be affected favourably by an independent Hungary. Palmerston, as we have seen, believed precisely the reverse. But the apathy and indifference so conspicuous outside governmental and parlia-mentary circles was mainly due to ignorance. Metternich was wrong when he said that Italy was only a geographical expression; it was certainly not a political entity, but it stood for whatever had been best in history and art and civilization. In the remotest of English provincial centres, the "cause" of Italy was easily comprehensible; but, for thousands of citizens—and these not the lowest class—on this side of the North Sea, the term "Hungary" was nothing more than the second half of a compound, and the Magyars were regarded as Austrian provincials. Enthusiasm at Pest or Debreczin for an independent Wales was about as likely as enthusiasm at London or Birmingham for an independent Hungary; or, considering the intelligent interest which so many Magyars took in lands remote from their own, perhaps much more likely. Even if an Englishman's geography and history were far above the average, it needed very close insight and very assiduous reading to understand what precisely the Magyar "cause" was. If the Latinity of the Pragmatic Sanction and the Laws of 1790-1 was matter of dispute at Pest, in England passion and eloquence for the Magyars could scarcely be expected. Over here, forensic subtlety has never been regarded as furnishing a just *casus belli*.

Before 1849 had run its course, all this had been completely altered, and the country had worked itself into a perfect frenzy for the Hungarians. This was only, however, when their cause had become quite hopeless, and when it appeared identified with the cause of humanity. Haynau's butcheries, the trial of Louis Batthyányi, and the public flogging by the military of high-born ladies—these were events of a nature to fan to white heat the passions of Upper Tooting and Tillicoultry. Most Englishmen are potential Palmerstons, and love nothing better

than to wax indignant over the inhumanity of the
foreigner; so, petitions poured into the Foreign Office
declaiming against the monsters who were masters
in Austria, while the series of Bluebooks on Convict
Discipline and Transportation, describing at the
length of several thousand pages a condition of
affairs in our Australasian colonies which might have
made Radetzky shudder and Schwarzenberg weep,
were left unread. But this demonstration of feeling
for the Hungarians during the summer months of
1849 was not solely due to the fact that the war had
ceased to be an affair of legality and become one of
sentiment. The country was much better informed
than it had been in the previous year, and this was
chiefly due to the efforts of Francis Pulszky. Perhaps,
as has been said, Szalay had written to Hungary
that until the English were better informed about
Foreign Affairs no help could be expected from that
quarter. Certain it is that Szalay's successor was to
busy himself, not with the Government, but with the
man in the street. England was a constitutional
country, and, if the English people could be taught
what the Magyars were really fighting for, and the
justice of that fight, then Downing Street must of
necessity take steps in favour of the Magyars[1].

---

[1] "Die ungarische Regierung entschloss sich nunmehr zu
einer anderen Taktik England gegenüber. Der Agitator sollte
dem Gesandten den Weg bahnen, die englische Regierung
sollte durch die öffentliche Meinung zu einer Stellungnahme
zugunsten Ungarns gezwungen werden. Diese Spekulation
war nicht unklug und nicht ganz ohne Berechtigung." Alter,
p. 100.

Quite at the end of the year 1848 Pulszky was commissioned to go to London, but not as a diplomatic agent. His chief task was to win over public opinion, and find out some way whereby a large consignment of weapons might be sent to Hungary[1]. The choice was one of the best Kossuth ever made, although he repented of it a short time afterwards. Pulszky, unlike so many of his colleagues, who were intended to gain hostile Governments and unsympathetic peoples for the Hungarian movement, was more than an amateur at the game of diplomacy. In Hungary he had already been Under-Secretary for Finance, and later Under-Secretary for Foreign Affairs. In addition, his intelligence was of a high order, his industry was amazing, and his personality not devoid of charm. Above all, he understood the art of treading warily. Teleki's moments of magnificent optimism, alternated with fits of black despair, were entirely alien to him; nor did the national vanity of a Kossuth lead him to the belief that Hungary was unconquerable, and that Europe would inevitably see to it that she was not conquered. He came to London at the end of February and, soon after, made that unofficial visit to Palmerston which has already been recorded, and the outcome of which was so disheartening to the Hungarians. But Pulszky had expected to find an apathetic Government, and set to work all the more zealously in his appointed province—the gaining of sympathy among the public.

---

[1] Pulszky, *Meine Zeit, mein Leben*, vol. II. p. 282. (Followed by Alter, p. 102.)

He soon had a group of talented English friends
devoting their journalistic efforts to the cause which
he represented. Chief of these were John Mitchell
Kemble, the historian of the Anglo-Saxons; Charles
Henningsen[1], a versatile and travelled man, who had
fought with Zumalacarreguy in Spain, and later became Kossuth's secretary; Francis Newman and
Toulmin Smith. Their campaign of publicity was far
more successful than Teleki's in Paris, and this, when
one considers the material with which the two agitators worked, is perhaps Pulszky's best claim to the
gratitude of his country. Among the papers which
printed the articles of Pulszky and his friends were
The Daily News, *Morning Advertiser*, *Spectator*,
Examiner, *Observer*, and even Palmerston's most
ardent champion in all Fleet Street, *The Globe*. In
addition to these were the popular Sunday papers,
and several provincial. But, although within a
month of his coming to England fourteen important
papers had opened their columns to him, Pulszky's
success was, after all, slight. *The Times* would have
nothing to do with him; Parliament—where his
most ardent champion was Lord Dudley Stuart—
was equally disappointing.

All the more radical members of the Government party
joined us; but they constantly proclaimed the non-intervention policy of England, both as regards Hungary and

---

[1] Pulszky wrongly calls him Hennigsen; see the British
Museum Catalogue: his chief literary effort was the description
of his year's campaigning in Spain. (See also his pamphlets
Kossuth and the 'Times,' 1851; and *The Past and Future of
Hungary*, 1852.)

the whole world, and they took no sort of steps to prevent the Russian intervention. They bestowed their pity both upon us and upon Austria; the latter they believed had taken a false path, which, unless it were abandoned betimes, must lead to her ruin, but they never promised us anything except good counsel and sympathy.

Precisely so; Palmerston's more radical friends held exactly the same views on the subject as the Foreign Secretary himself. And what Lord Eddisbury had written to Szalay, concerning the international position of Hungary, was repeated in a still more practical manner, and from another quarter, to Pulszky. Kossuth had concluded an agreement with the Fiume shipbuilding firm of Matkovics for the purchase of a frigate, which was to secure that harbour to the Hungarians, notwithstanding the Croatian insurrection, and to facilitate the importation of armaments by sea into the country. The frigate was built in Fiume, and then taken to London to be equipped as a vessel of war. While it was still in England, however, Windischgrätz entered Pest, and Matkovics either through fear or for some other reason, handed it over to the Austrian Embassy in London, which straightway proceeded to confiscate it. The approval of the English Government had been given to this step, and therefore Pulszky was instructed to seek restitution through the law-courts, whose independence of the executive was a matter of European knowledge, and was indeed regarded by many continental publicists as the chief safe-guard of the English Constitution. What a German camarilla had denied was to be obtained in a place where justice and equity spoke out fearlessly. Pulszky, accordingly, laid the original of the agreement between the Hungarian Government and Matkovics before several eminent London lawyers, friends of his: could the frigate be reclaimed for his Government on such a ground? Their opinion was unanimous. A sovereign independent Hungary was not, and could not be, recognised, especially as the Austrian Government not only in law, but in fact, was master of the land, although perhaps for the moment a portion of the Hungarian territory had withdrawn its allegiance from this master. The Hungarian Government represented the insurrection, not the land, and no English tribunal could possibly dispute or invalidate the confiscation of the vessel by the Austrian Government, which legally was also the Government of Hungary. Pulszky dared not, after this, take the matter into the courts[1].

More discouragement followed for him after the Declaration of Independence of April 14th, for the English were very much out of humour with it. A certain Colonel Bikkesy was sent as special envoy to London with the original declaration, which was translated for him by Pulszky, who spoke English quite fluently. He was, also, instrumental in bringing

[1] Pulszky, vol. II. pp. 332–33—not p. 323, as Alter asserts. The latter (pp. 103–5) gives some details which are not in Pulszky's account; he christens the vessel "Kossuth," and condemns her to "*ein unrühmliches Ende als Baumwollschiff*," apparently following official English and Austrian sources, which I have not seen.

about a meeting between the Colonel and Palmerston in the private house of the Foreign Secretary, who, however, "recognised the Declaration of Independence simply as an interesting document." In the letter[1] in which Bikkesy sent this Declaration (July 19th, 1849) was, also, enclosed " a Declaration of the principles on which the Government of Hungary is ready to regulate its policy as regards its commercial regulations with Great Britain." This document, " taking for its provisional basis the most favourable tariff," was to be not only a witness of the "amicable feeling with which the Government of Hungary is animated towards the Government of Her Majesty," but also a "pledge of its intention, when the affairs of the country are definitely arranged, to adopt the most liberal commercial principles." The statement of the tariff—incredibly concise for one of Kossuth's official documents—if, on the one hand, it did offer very real commercial advantages to England, was to be equally useful to the hard-pressed and fugitive Government:

English goods will enjoy provisionally the same advantages granted heretofore to Austrian goods imported into Hungary. Articles of commerce rendered necessary by the actual state of Hungary, such as arms (including sabres, bayonets, weapons and saddlery), cloth, canvas, leather, ready-made shoes for soldiers, etc., shall be free of duty; and, as regards arms, bounties shall even be given.

Had the English Government been actually willing to negotiate, and so depart from its former attitude of

[1] *Correspondence*, No. 234.

the most correct neutrality, it is difficult to imagine
how a considerable trade could have been carried on,
when the Magyars saw themselves constrained to
conduct their foreign affairs from Paris, and were lucky
if they could manage to get a bundle of despatches
sent off by the anything but safe overland route via
Constantinople. In point of fact, not even a bare
acknowledgment by the Under-secretary of the
receipt of Bikkesy's letter appears in the Bluebook;
and if, as has been asserted, one of the motives which
prompted Kossuth to the Declaration of Independence was the desire to give to his Government an
international standing which sympathetic but scrupulously correct statesmen at Paris and London could
recognise, he was doomed to disappointment; as, also,
was his repeated attempt to appeal to the English
on the strongest of grounds, the pocket. Shortly
after Bikkesy's mission, Kasimir Batthyányi, the
Hungarian Minister for Foreign Affairs, sent to
Pulszky his credentials for the English Government.
But his friends told him that even *private* intercourse would be broken off if he claimed an official
position, and he made no attempt to hand in his
credentials. In the Bluebook are only two letters
from Pulszky to Palmerston, and the second of these
bears a date two days subsequent to Görgei's
surrender at Világos.

"My task," says the Hungarian, "could therefore
only be that of recruiting more and more friends for
the Hungarian cause, so that our Government, in case
we should one day be victorious, might be actually
recognised."

As a recruiting-sergeant he was certainly not a failure, and, as has been mentioned, the outburst of pro-Magyar sympathy in England in the late summer of 1849 was to a large extent due to his efforts and those of his friends. His original home in London had been a boarding-house in Golden Square; but it was pointed out to him that the "representative of the interests of Hungary" must, if he was to do good work in English society, find a more ambitious residence. He therefore migrated, perforce, to Jermyn Street, that home of younger sons of peers and M.P.'s who had left their wives in the country; although, as he adds with a note of humorous regret, Cardinal Wiseman had not been too proud to live opposite to the boarding-house in Golden Square. In spite of Jermyn Street, Pulszky won over but few of the upper ten thousand; among the upper middle classes, however, the liberal professions and the learned world—he was once a well-known figure in the British Museum reading-room—he gained numerous friends for himself and his country. His recruits among the newspaper-reading public in and outside London must have numbered very many thousands. His mission is certainly one of the most interesting episodes of the Hungarian struggle for independence[1].

[1] The above sketch of Pulszky's mission in London is based on the account towards the end of the second volume of his autobiography, cited above. That account has been condemned as worthless; but I can see no reason for such a condemnation. Wherever possible, I have tested the accuracy of his statement, and have come across nothing worse than slips of memory,

If it is clear from the history of the Hungarian missions in London that Palmerston never intended to aid the revolted Hungarians in any sort of manner, the Foreign Office records point still more irresistibly to the same conclusion. In fact, until after Világos the "affairs of Hungary" troubled him very little; then, as will be seen, he took up their cause vigorously enough. At that late hour it was partly a question of humanity, partly of diplomacy and the Balance of Power, partly of Sir Stratford Canning's initiative, partly—perhaps chiefly—of public opinion. For Palmerston is in one sense closely akin to Louis Kossuth; he is the British statesman, *par excellence*, of public opinion. Unlike the Hungarian, he was never carried away by the voice of the multitude, never led to take up a line of conduct which he himself did not hold to be right or the best, merely because the clamour of Demos declared it right and the best. But if it was possible to walk in the sunshine of popular favour without ignoring the path of duty, then Palmerston would do so. Thus it comes about that as democratic passions mount at Tooting, and vituperation waxes more riotous at Notting Hill, the despatches from the Foreign Office become more and more outspoken and the advice

and one or two mistakes in orthography, which may be his or his printer's. He is, certainly, not boastful, and what he says of Palmerston is confirmed by everything else that I have been able to discover. The account of the mission given above is carried only as far as the Russian intervention, because it is desirable to treat the diplomatic campaign against that intervention as a connected whole.

less and less palatable. The Austrians deserved it, and Hungary had been preserved to them, which was Palmerston's chief concern.

All this was very hard on Ponsonby, the Ambassador at Vienna, who was in his element at the Hofburg and at Schönbrunn, and who saw in the Hungarian movement merely an attempt "at the advancement of the new French system[1]." Even a Stratford Canning, had he been at Vienna, would have found it embarrassing to read some of Palmerston's despatches to the Austrian Government; but for Lord Ponsonby it must have been heart-breaking. Palmerston finally lost all patience with him, and wrote the private letter printed in Ashley's biography:

I write you this, and desire you to do your best, though I hear from many quarters that you oppose instead of furthering the policy of your Government; and that you openly declare that you disapprove of our course. No diplomat ought to hold such language as long as he holds his appointment. It is idle trash to say that we are hostile to Austria because we may disapprove of the policy of a Metternich, or the cruelties of the Manning administration which now governs Austria; you might as well say that a man is the enemy of his friend because he tells that friend of errors and faults which are sinking him in the esteem of men whose good opinion is worth having[2].

Pridham, an English traveller in Austria-Hungary at the time, had an opportunity of hearing Ponsonby's

---

[1] Ponsonby to Palmerston, May 5th, 1848.

[2] Ashley, *Life of Palmerston*, vol. II. p. 122, Ed. 1879, Nov. 27th, 1849, i.e. during a critical period of the Refugees Question.

views, and has, also, left it on record that the ideas
of the Ambassador were decidedly not those which
seemed to animate the Foreign Office. Blackwell,
the secret agent, tells the same tale. But the Ambassador must not be judged too harshly. Metternich
and the rest of them could be very charming in
private life, and, if Ponsonby's politics were less
progressive than those of his chief, it is good to read
of him that, during the troubled times of 1848, he
was the calmest and most imperturbable of men.
When Windischgrätz bombarded Vienna, the Englishman was the last to leave the city, walking "com-
posedly through the Kärnthner Thor[1]." But his
despatches are very dull reading, and add absolutely
nothing to our knowledge of the Viennese or Hungarian Revolutions; when one remembers the volume
of Lord Gower's despatches, and Ponsonby's opportunities of seeing and knowing, one perceives how
insignificant his contribution to the history of the
Völkerfrühling really is. His reports are, in fact,
neither more nor less than what he heard in Government circles, and what he got out of the inspired
periodicals: the official language of Viennese bureau-
crats rendered still more uninspiring by a blend of
Ponsonby's own particular brand of diplomatic
persiflage. Palmerston made matters worse when he
compiled the *Correspondence on the Affairs of Hungary*. Ponsonby held strong personal views on the
work and character of Kossuth, and when he ex-

[1] Lord Augustus Loftus, *Diplomatic Reminiscences*, vol. I.
p. 129.

pounds these views the despatches begin to be interesting; but Palmerston, out of respect for the fame of Ponsonby, or of Kossuth, or of both, pitilessly excised these passages when the papers were laid on the table of the House. But it is with Palmerston's despatches to Ponsonby that we are chiefly concerned. His lack of sympathy for the Hungarian cause, and his real views, are seen in the absence of such despatches. While he daily compiled long and eloquent sermons on the affairs of Italy, he wrote, during the whole of 1848, only two brief Notes touching Hungarian matters, which he thought worthy of inclusion in the Bluebook. The earlier of these states, if somewhat perfunctorily, a genuine desire, and ends with the true Palmerstonian parting sting:

It is much to be wished that the Austrian Government may be able to pursue a course of policy which may keep together and reunite in a closer and firmer manner those discordant elements of the Austrian Empire whose differences seem at present to threaten it with dissolution. But such a result can hardly be accomplished, as some persons about the Court of Vienna seem to think, by military force alone[1].

The second merely enclosed a copy of Eddisbury's letter of December 13th to Szalay[2]. The same is true as to the early months of 1849, in fact, until the Hungarians had been beaten and their cause was becoming popular in England. Once again, the Italian despatches are legion.

[1] Palmerston to Ponsonby, Sept. 29th, 1848. *Correspondence*, No. 47.
[2] *Correspondence*, No. 79.

The only despatch of this period which possesses any interest is one dated July 2nd, ordering Mr Blackwell to resume his duties as agent for Her Majesty's Government. Blackwell had served both Aberdeen and Palmerston in a non-diplomatic character in Hungary. His reports on the work of the Diet of 1847-8—printed in the *Correspondence*—are of especial merit and interest, and he was a far more intelligent observer, and acute judge, of events and men than Lord Ponsonby. His sympathies were frankly pro-Magyar, and he was *persona grata* at Pest; but many of his reports are wonderfully unbiased. He, like so many contemporaries, misjudged the amazing recuperative powers of Austria, and wrote to Palmerston to warn him against bolstering up the sick man of Vienna:

I must observe that an opinion begins to prevail here at Pest that H.M. Government is determined to maintain the integrity of the Austrian Empire, even at the risk of a European war. I trust that such an opinion is totally without foundation, being convinced that this Empire is already virtually dissolved, and that no power on earth will be able to reconstitute it[1].

His chief desire was to be appointed Consul-General at Pest, a desire not wholly alien to the Hungarian Cabinet, but which Palmerston, of course, did not fulfil. To Blackwell also the Hungarian Ministers

---

[1] Blackwell to Palmerston, April 25th, 1848; in Ponsonby's despatch of May 7th; an extract from this report is printed in the Bluebook (No. 21) but the most interesting passages are omitted.

disburdened their intentions with regard to their alliances:

The Premier Count Louis Batthyányi then proceeded to say that I was perfectly aware that Hungary was now to all intents and purposes an independent kingdom and that in their political and commercial policy, the Hungarian ministers would of course only take into consideration the interests of Hungary. On the supposition that the Austrian Hereditary States would be incorporated in the renascent Germanic Empire, and that Lombardy and Galicia must eventually be abandoned, he observed, that the question arose whether Hungary should look for support to Germany or to England. He, for his own part, preferred England, for a hundred reasons which it was unnecessary to state; but "the British Government must show some signs of life" (I give his own words), "must show, by the speedy appointment of a Consul-General, that England is aware of the political as well as the commercial importance of Hungary.... It is" concluded the Premier "my firm conviction that the moral support of England is all that we require. If this support be afforded, the discordant social element of our country will be speedily neutralised; but if the British Government should hesitate—should continue to be ignorant of Hungary as an independent kingdom, we must look to the Germans, and strive to render our political and commercial interests compatible with those of the German Confederation[1]."

Klauzál, who held the portfolio of Trade, Agriculture and Manufacturing Industry, and was substantially a Free-trader, spoke in a similar strain to Blackwell.

[1] Blackwell to Palmerston, April 25th, 1848. The passages given above are omitted in the Bluebook.

The allusion to the *Zollverein* was a clever idea, for Palmerston's dislike to that union must have been known both to Blackwell and Batthyányi; but the appeal—as has been seen—to our commercial interests was fruitless. More than a year later, after the Declaration of Independence, and when the Russian intervention was a certainty, Blackwell wrote with an undercurrent of bitterness, that in April 1848 the Hungarians only desired the *moral* support of England, which, if granted, would in all human probability have prevented war. But that support at that time had not been forthcoming[1].

On July 2nd, 1849, Palmerston ordered Blackwell to resume his mission; but he was not to reside in Hungary this time:

...in the present state of things H.M. Government do not think it expedient that Mr Blackwell should go to Hungary. His presence there as a person sent to make reports to the British Government would be liable to misconstruction by both parties engaged in the war. The Austrian Government might consider it as an unfriendly proceeding, calculated to give encouragement to the Hungarians, and the Hungarians might view it in the same light, and might found upon it expectations of assistance and support which, as H.M. Government do not intend to take any part in the contest, would be disappointed: and the Hungarians might therefore, if their affairs should go ill, found upon Mr Blackwell's mission complaints that they had been misled by the British Government and had been induced by false

[1] Blackwell to Palmerston, May 11th, 1849. Dated from 4, Charles Street, Clarendon Square.

hopes of assistance to neglect opportunities of coming to terms by negotiation[1].

Blackwell was therefore to reside at Graz in Styria, and to refrain from any proceedings which might appear to identify him with either belligerent.

The Russian intervention in the summer of 1849 came as a surprise to nobody, either on the Continent or in Great Britain. It was common knowledge, as de Tocqueville said, that Nicholas had "made for himself, out of the cause of authority throughout the world, a second Empire yet vaster than the first." There were, indeed, a score of reasons why the Czar should save the Dual Monarchy from utter disintegration; of these, some were dictated by policy, and motives of self-interest, some by that truly imperial generosity which, as no historian has yet denied, was one of the autocrat's chief characteristics.

"When Nicholas I offered his aid," says Dr Friedjung, "he was partly moved by the consideration that the victory of the Hungarian Revolution would have for its immediate consequence the falling away of Poland from Russia, since several thousand Poles were serving in the Hungarian Army. This, however, was not his prime motive. For he regarded himself as the guardian of the monarchical and conservative cause in Europe, and had, in addition, at his meeting with the Emperor Francis at Münchengrätz in 1833 vowed to the latter that he would stand by his son under every circumstance. With all his

[1] Palmerston to Mr Magenis, July 2nd, 1849. Magenis was Chargé d'Affaires at Vienna during Lord Ponsonby's absence in May, June and the first half of July, 1849. Blackwell's mission ceased October 31st, 1849.

severity, Nicholas was, after his kind, an idealist; otherwise, he would never have set on foot, for the sake of an
alien cause, a considerable army, without claiming in
return the slightest aid from Austria. Common prudence
demanded that he should at the same time assure himself
of the consent of the Viennese Cabinet tó an attempt on
Constantinople; but he gave himself up to the belief that
the Austria which he had saved would never deny to him
this proof of gratitude. The common campaign against
Hungary was agreed upon as a family affair between the
two reigning houses; Nicholas behaved as the fatherly
friend of his youthful neighbour: and Schwarzenberg,
without possessing a single vein of sentiment, understood
how to keep this feeling awake, through the medium of the
ladies of the Imperial house of Austria[1]."

The above account is perhaps a little too unqualified;
in spite of the genuine and deep-rooted desire to
protect his "youthful neighbour," the Czar probably did, at any rate, attempt to stipulate for some
return on account of the magnificent service he was
rendering to the Austrian monarchy. The English
Consul-General at Warsaw, Colonel du Plat, wrote
to Palmerston on June 2nd an account of an interview
between Nicholas, the Chancellor Nesselrode and
General Daehn. The Czar had demanded Daehn's
opinion on the

incorporation of Galicia with the Kingdom of Poland,
with the view of better keeping down (*comprimer*) for
the future, Polish turbulence with the strong hand and
iron will of the Emperor.

[1] Friedjung, *op. cit.* vol. I. p. 216.

Daehn had replied that such a scheme would demand too many soldiers, and would involve too great an expense.

"I should ask for Cracow, for the Salt Mines of Wieliczka, and for certain districts lying between those two places; with a few small parcels of territory, to obtain a better military frontier for the present Kingdom of Poland: by such an arrangement it might be possible even to diminish the Army usually kept in Poland, and the Exchequer would benefit at the rate of some nine or ten millions of florins (about £250,000) annually, which are now paid to Austria for salt." I understood that the Emperor appeared to approve this view; but His Majesty did not express any opinion[1].

Whether this interview really took place or not is by no means certain. Du Plat's authority for it was perhaps not of the best. It would appear, however, to be safe to assert that nothing was definitely settled in black and white between the two monarchs regarding the Czar's future policy towards the Ottoman Empire.

Nor was the intervention altogether unconnected with the affairs of Germany. Once reestablished in her pristine might, and again, as of old, the bulwark of conservatism, Austria, Nicholas thought, would be able to combat the building-up of a united Germany; or, at any rate, she would be able to prevent its having a democratic basis. A strong Germany on his western frontier could in no case be pleasing to the Czar; but a strong Germany, the foundations of which

[1] Colonel du Plat to Palmerston, June 2nd, 1849.

were rooted in revolution, would be as absolutely
detestable as an independent Hungary and an independent Poland.

"The Russians," wrote the English Chargé d'Affaires
in St Petersburg, "look forward, by speedily relieving the
Austrian Government of the embarrassments of the
Hungarian War—to enable them to act with greater
decision and energy in the affairs of Germany; and it is
evidently contemplated that Austria will, ere long, have
an opportunity of recovering what is here considered to
be her legitimate influence in that country, and of com-
bating the revolutionary projects of the republican and
anarchical party in the smaller states of the Confederation,
by employing her own forces for that purpose, while she
may leave her territories under the protection of the
advanced guard of the Russian armies[1]."

Finally, as already hinted, the Russian statesmen
wished to show the Slavs of the Dual Monarchy, to
whom they had to look for aid and protection in their
hour of need. The intervention was in this respect no
more than a stone in the great Panslav edifice which
they were erecting at St Petersburg[2].

The Hungarians believed that England and France
must do something at last. Twelve months of failure
at Paris and London had taught them that the
Western Powers were not prepared to sacrifice a
single man for the Independence of Hungary. In
May 1849, however, it was no longer a question of

---

[1] Andrew Buchanan to Palmerston, May 10th, 1849. Lord
Bloomfield, the English Ambassador in St Petersburg, was
on leave of absence in this country at the time.
[2] Blackwell to Palmerston, Oct. 5th, 1849.

the independence or subjugation of Hungary merely, but of the naked and avowed aggrandisement of Russia towards the west. England, whose great object of dread was that expansion, which would upset the Balance of Power, must now see how European liberties were in truth bound up with the Magyar cause; and the most scrupulously correct of statesmen might safely throw overboard the policy of non-intervention, in the face of so great a departure from that policy by the enemy. Moreover, Turkey was now quite definitely threatened, and, with Turkey, the commercial interests of England in the Near East, and ultimately her empire beyond Persia and the Himalayas: it was a fundamental maxim of the Foreign Office that India must be defended on the shores of the Bosphorus[1].

On April 17th, Blackwell, at that time resident in London, reported to Palmerston the views of the moderate men in Hungary, who were already seeking the friendly mediation of England.

My correspondents in Hungary belong to the party of Moderate Liberals, or what the French would term the Left Centre. This party—the most influential in Hungary —is sincerely desirous of settling the disputes with Austria, through the mediation of H.M. Government. If the Austrian ministers wish to avoid involving Europe in a general war by demanding the aid of Russia, I should imagine that they would *now* (after the recent victories of the Hungarians) gladly avail themselves of any overture which Your Lordship might deem it advisable to make to them.

[1] Pulszky, *op. cit.* vol. II. p. 336.

I have reason to believe that the Hungarians, or at least the party alluded to, would consent to an arrangement on the following terms:

1st. The Kingdom of Hungary to consist of Hungary proper: that is to say, Hungary north of the river Drave, and Transylvania.

2nd. Croatia, Slavonia, with their military frontiers, and Dalmatia to be constituted as the representatives of those provinces might decide at a Diet to meet for the purpose at Agram.

3rd. Hungary to have a port on the Adriatic—either on the Hungarian Littoral or in Istria—with the right of road to it; in the same manner as Austria has a right of road through the Bavarian territories from Salzburg to the Tyrol: a right which, if I be not mistaken, is guaranteed by the Treaties of 1815....

I have ventured to make this communication to Your Lordship, from the conviction that if the disputes between Austria and Hungary be not *speedily* settled by the amicable mediation of a Foreign Power, a European war is unavoidable, and from my considering myself in some measure authorised to express an opinion respecting the affairs of Hungary, with which I ought at least to be thoroughly acquainted.

I am perfectly aware that my views...differ materially from those of Her Majesty's ambassador at Vienna[1].

A few weeks later he wrote again. He had not, he stated, had knowledge of the Declaration of Independence when writing his last letter. But the Hungarians would still accept British mediation on the terms stated in that letter, if the Russian intervention could be avoided. Had Szalay, he continued,

[1] Blackwell to Palmerston, April 17th, 1849.

been able to manage an interview with Palmerston when in England, he was to have made a similar proposal. If the Austrians declined the mediation of Great Britain, and the arms of the Hungarians were successful, then they "would be inclined to place a member of the Coburg-Kohary family on the throne, provided they could calculate on his being recognised by England." The time for mediation had, indeed, gone by; but Palmerston might still exercise a salutary influence without compromising Her Majesty's Government. Such influence, if the Hungarians were successful, would suffice to determine the form of government and, if this were monarchical, the person to be chosen King[1].

At Debreczin, when they knew that the Czar's assistance had been definitely requested and as definitely promised, they began the campaign against the imminent peril by investing their agent in London with a diplomatic character. The time was now come for Pulszky to turn from the man in the street to Palmerston in Downing Street. In the letter which contained the nomination of Francis Pulszky as Chargé d'Affaires of Great Britain and Ireland, was enclosed a note to Palmerston on the Russian intervention:

I hope that Your Excellency, faithful to your just and liberal policy, will not be indifferent to such an infraction of the law of nations, and that you will interpose the powerful protest of Great Britain to prevent it.

[1] Blackwell to Palmerston, May 11th, 1849.

At the same time, it was pointed out to Pulszky how
the intervention must infallibly upset the Balance
of Power, and the new Chargé d'Affaires was instructed to obtain from Great Britain a recognition
of the right of the Hungarian Government to communicate freely with other Governments, and a
protest so solemn against the intervention that the
first step of a Russian soldier on Hungarian soil
would be regarded as nothing less than a *casus belli*[1].
To make assurance doubly sure, the Hungarian
Cabinet were prepared for great sacrifices, as they
still believed that, if the price offered were great
enough, the Foreign Office would have to surrender
to the demands of the mercantile and trading classes.
To this end they were ready to sacrifice that territorial integrity of their country, the inviolable
maintenance of which had been one of the chief
paragraphs in the programme of revolution. In this
sense Kasimir Batthyányi wrote to Pulszky from
Debreczin, on May 19th, that, if necessary, the Hungarian Government were prepared to offer Semlin to
England, which would assure to the latter the commercial preponderance on the Lower Danube. If a
strong place on the Adriatic were demanded in addition, the harbour of Buccari would serve. These
cessions would naturally depend on the course of

[1] *Foreign Office Records*, F.O. 7, 375, May 15th, 1849.
Contained in a letter from Pulszky dated August 16th, but
not in the Bluebook. In that volume is printed a letter from
Pulszky to Palmerston of the same date (No. 298), containing
a rhetorical protest against the intervention and the perjured
House of Habsburg-Lorraine.

negotiations and the ultimate sanction of the Hungarian Government; in any case, they could be realised only on one condition: "if we in return can obtain the actual armed protest of England against the Russian intervention." Hungary was, also, prepared to enter into a commercial treaty with England, the basis of which should go beyond the "most favoured nation" tariff which Bikkesy had been instructed to offer; for, according to the new scheme, English trade was to enjoy more advantages in Hungary than Austria had formerly enjoyed. The letter concludes with a passionate appeal to Pulszky to take almost any steps, if he could but secure the energetic protest of the British Government against the Russian intervention.

I believe that England—according to her earlier utterances—will not tolerate this insolent violation of all natural rights. The arrival of an English fleet in the Dardanelles would make us sure of Turkey; but why could not England, in order to make a really emphatic protest, send a fleet into the Baltic[1]?

Palmerston, doubtless, received this letter (although it is not to be found in the Foreign Office records), for Pulszky had powerful friends in England, and, in addition, ample means of seeing Palmerston privately.

When the Western Powers still maintained silence, and after the main Russian army had crossed the

[1] Batthyányi to Palmerston: Debreczin, May 19th, 1849. Printed in the collection of Batthyányi's *Official Letters* to Pulszky, at the end of vol. II. of Pulszky's autobiography. This collection is not complete.

frontier, the passion of appeal was converted into
the passion of menace, and the Hungarian Government threatened to toss the firebrand of Revolution
into the magazine of the nations. Such is the argument of the Circular Note of June 25th, which
Kasimir Batthyányi addressed to the Hungarian
agents abroad:

> The tinder is in our hands, and, if it be necessary to fire
> it off, we shall only take counsel for our own safety; and
> it may easily come to pass, that the barbarian of the
> North shall live to see a second burning of Moscow,
> which will consume more than the dead walls of a city[1].

Still later, when the Hungarians were in a yet more
desperate position, a final attempt was made to
purchase the help of England in a letter dated
Szegedin, July 14th, and written in Batthyányi's
hand throughout, which probably did not reach
Pulszky until after Hungary lay at the feet of the
Czar. If England would take steps to assure the
national independence of Hungary, Kossuth and
Batthyányi would, in their turn, attempt to bring
about the recognition by the Magyars of a King pro-
posed by England, who should be a member of the
deposed dynasty, but not Francis Joseph. "But
now or never!" There follows a still more amazing
proposition: if England were not opposed to such
a scheme, Turkey, the Turkish protectorates and
Hungary might together compose a union of states

[1] Alter, pp. 175–6; the text of the note is in Korn, *Kossuth
und die Ungarn in der Türkei* (Hamburg and New York, 1851),
pp. 20 *et seq*.

(*Staatsverband*), of which Turkey should be the head, and which should be quite capable of taking Austria's place in the family of nations. Hungary would, of course, preserve her national independence; and England would have the opportunity of putting the policy of Russia to shame, and of securing a position in the Near East such as she had never had before. The integrity of Turkey would be guaranteed for years; while to England would fall the choice of the form of government and of the person at the head of a new kingdom, which would be a market for her trade, and a rich source of increase to her material and political power[1].

Doubtless, Pulszky was too little of a political idealist to hand this letter over to Palmerston, even supposing he received it before the surrender at Világos had robbed it of whatever practical worth it may originally have possessed. But to the historian it is of the greatest interest. It shows that Kossuth and his Foreign Secretary at last understood what

[1] Count Kasimir Batthyányi to Pulszky, July 14th, 1849. In the appendix to Pulszky, vol. II., Alter (p. 186) asserts that the Turkish Grand Vizier Reshid Pasha was pleased with the idea; but that England, who saw that it would put the whole of the Balkans in a blaze, and did not hesitate a moment to point out its dangers to Turkey, repeated her admonitions to neutrality, and declared that in case of war Turkey must not expect her support. As his authorities for this, he cites despatches from Canning to Palmerston and from Palmerston to Canning, which do not exist. Although there is no mention of the scheme in Canning's despatches, Batthyányi, in his letter, states positively that it was Canning's: "So much I know; Sir Stratford Canning, to quieten the English Government, has set this as a condition for the recognition of our independence."

exactly Palmerston meant when he spoke of Austria
as a European necessity, and of the impossibility of
preserving the Balance of Power if small independent
states were substituted in its place. Amongst these
states Palmerston reckoned Hungary. But the
argument did not apply, if Austria's place were to be
taken, not by an isolated Hungary, but by a powerful
Balkan Confederation, stretching from the Carpa-
thians to Constantinople, from Fiume to the Black
Sea. with the inexhaustible Asiatic hinterland to
draw upon in case of need. Such a Confederation,
young and vigorous, while Austria was old and effete,
animated by the fiercest hostility against Russia in
place of Austrian subservience to that Power, and, in
extent of territory and population incomparably
superior to the dominions of Francis Joseph—such
a Confederation must for Palmerston's policy in the
Near East, surely, seem worth half a dozen Austrias[1].

[1] Alter, p. 191, speaks of yet another attempt to gain the
assistance of England. "A short time afterwards, after the
failure of the plan to let England stand godmother to the
Danubian Empire under the suzerainty of Turkey, Kossuth
had taken steps to offer the crown to a member of the English
royal family. Kossuth, indeed, thought that he must make a
better offer to the proud dynasty of England than to the
modest House of Coburg-Kohary; and thus, in the last days
of July, Count Teleki was commissioned to repair to London
as special envoy of the Hungarian Government, and not only
once more to offer to the English Government the monopoly
of trade in Hungary, but also to invite Prince Arthur, a
younger son of Queen Victoria, to accept the crown of the
triune kingdom of Hungary, Croatia and Dalmatia—a
dominion which therefore would include, not only the lands
of the crown of St Stephen, but also a piece of Austrian
territory." Of these posthumous papers of Cobden I know
nothing; the account in Korn differs from that in Alter, and

But, however great the sacrifices which the Hungarians were prepared to make, they were sacrifices to an unheeding Power. Palmerston, who had underrated the force of the Hungarian movement during the closing months of 1848, in the spring of 1849 saw the very existence of the Austrian Empire threatened. The Russians alone could save it; so the Russians should save it, and meet with no protest from the Foreign Office. He had little fear for the future. Gratitude is seldom a decisive factor in diplomacy, and the memory of Austrian statesmen was proverbially short. The rescued Viennese

is, obviously, not true. He says that the Court of St James' was not altogether averse from the proposal to make Prince Arthur king of the "noble Hungarian nation," and continues: "This, together with the uncertainty as to what claims Russia would put forward, if she succeeded in suppressing Hungary, induced the English Minister of Foreign Affairs to allow traces to appear of the possibility of a recognition of Hungarian independence." Korn gives no date, except the general indication: "at the time of the Russian invasion of Hungary." Philipp Korn, formerly commandant of the Kaschau division of the German Legion in Hungary, lived for a year with Kossuth and the refugees in Turkey. His book was published in 1851, and dedicated to Theresa Pulszky. It will be observed that Alter purges Korn's account of the most glaring mistakes: one would like to see the cited paper by Cobden. The date given by Alter would make the offer of the Crown to Prince Arthur coincident with, or earlier than, the offer contained in the letter of July 14th, which assigned to England the disposal of the Hungarian Crown, but added that the choice must fall on a Habsburg. A long list of Teleki's letters is printed in Pulszky, vol. II.; but there is nothing at all corresponding to Alter's "commission" in the closing days of July. Doubtless, there was some talk of offering the crown of St Stephen to a member of the English royal house—as it was certainly offered to other royal houses— and Korn confounded this with the actual proposal made in the letter of July 14th.

Government would soon perceive that the sometime rescuer was the eternal enemy, and would shape its policy accordingly[1]. Palmerston's despatches leave no room for doubt on this point.

"Much as Her Majesty's Government regret this interference of Russia," he wrote to Buchanan on May 17th, "the causes which have led to it, and the effects which it may produce, they nevertheless have not considered the occasion to be one which at present calls for any formal expression of the opinions of Great Britain on the matter[2]."

To Colonel du Plat he was still more laconic and to the point; that most conscientious of Consul-Generals was forbidden to express any opinion whatever on the contest in progress between Austria and Hungary, or upon the Russian intervention. "The British Government are spectators to those events, and neither parties to, nor judges of, them[3]." The Chargé d'Affaires at Vienna was not even honoured with a special despatch on the subject; he received for his instruction nothing more than copies of the Russian Circular on the intervention (which repre-

[1] "The English ministers were indeed very indignant at the Russian intervention and foresaw that it would lead to a Turkish war. Yet they took no action which might have weakened the Austrian Monarchy; for they regarded it as a safe ally in the Eastern Question, and knew only too well that there is no such thing as gratitude in politics, and that in the end interests always gained the victory over feelings." Pulszky, vol. II. p. 338.

[2] Palmerston to Buchanan, May 17th, 1849, *Correspondence*, No. 179.

[3] Palmerston to du Plat, May 24th, 1849.

sented it as a matter of self-defence), and of the despatch of May 17th to Buchanan[1].

But the whole policy of Palmerston is most clearly seen in the correspondence which passed between him and the cleverest of all the English diplomatic agents abroad. To trace this policy, it will be necessary to go back to a date about twelve months prior to the Russian intervention in Hungary. In June 1848, the very month when Canning took up his fifth residence at Constantinople, disturbances broke out in the two Danubian Principalities, Moldavia and Wallachia. There was real justification for the discontent of the inhabitants; and a few wise concessions would have restored order and set all to rights. These the Porte, under Canning's guidance, was quite willing to sanction; but Russia claimed that the stipulations of the Treaty of Adrianople gave to her, also, the right to preserve order in the Principalities; and, when Turkey, in opposition to Canning's advice to avoid a military occupation of the provinces, despatched troops across the Danube, 4000 Russians entered Moldavia. In a short time, the inhabitants were groaning under a huge army which they had to support at their own cost. Although the Russian Government claimed in their Circular on the occupation of the Principalities that they had entered with the consent of the Porte, their views as to the measures which should be taken for the restoration of tranquillity differed *toto coelo* from those of the Turkish statesmen.

[1] Palmerston to Magenis, *Correspondence*, No. 185.

"Turkey," says Mr Lane-Poole, "moved by the strenuous counsels of the British Ambassador, was for mild measures, amnesty to the 'reformers,' liberal amendments in the Constitution, and the speedy removal of the Russian troops. The Czar, on the other hand, imperiously demanded a severe repression of the 'revolution,' punishment of the 'rebels,' repudiation of free institutions, and a prolonged joint occupation in the interests of order. It was the old contest between the principles of the Holy Alliance and the liberal policy of George Canning[1]."

Sir Stratford saw in the affair yet another milestone on the road from St Petersburg to Constantinople, especially when he learned that Russia was seeking for an intimate alliance with the Porte. When the Turkish statesmen pressed for a defensive alliance with England, he was, without doubt, disappointed that Palmerston did not close with the idea at once. At St Petersburg they affected great regret at what had taken place, and disclaimed all ideas of aggrandisement. From the nature of the Czar's relations with Turkey, it was impossible to "avoid cooperating with the Ottoman forces"; and radicalism must be suppressed on their own frontiers. "*Nous l'avons fait à notre corps défendant*," said Nesselrode[2]. When Palmerston had heard Nesselrode's explanation, he replied as follows to Bloomfield:

H.M. Government place entire confidence in the declaration and assurance which the imperial Government has given in regard to this event; and H.M. Government entertain no doubt that the Government of Russia will

[1] *Life of Sir Stratford Canning*, vol. II. p. 178.
[2] Lord Bloomfield to Palmerston, July 18th, 1848.

avail themselves of the earliest opportunity which the course of events may afford them to withdraw their troops from the Principalities, and to replace them within the Russian frontier[1].

It soon became evident that an early evacuation could not be hoped for; and, as the winter passed away, the boasted concord and cooperation of the two occupying Powers gave place to a state of affairs which did not seem far removed from a Russo-Turkish war. Sir Stratford Canning became more and more alarmed, and urged Palmerston to prepare himself for the worst. The latter, of course, was frankly on the side of Turkey in the matter, and it was doubtless chiefly due to him that the French Government also made representations in the same spirit. But his behaviour throughout, in spite of a little sharp language now and then, betrays quite unwonted complaisance[2]. In fact, he believed that one of the main aims of the Russian movement in the Danubian Principalities was the ultimate lending of assistance to Austria against the Hungarians, and that the Czar's eyes, for the time being were, not on

[1] Palmerston to Bloomfield, Aug. 2nd, 1848. See also the debate in the Commons of March 22nd, 1849. Palmerston said that "he was confident that the Russian Government had no intention of making a permanent encroachment on the Turkish Empire." It was a question of time, not of ulterior intentions. Hansard, CIII. pp. 1128 *et seq*.

[2] "*Pourquoi l'Angleterre témoigne-t-elle, en présence de l'occupation des provinces danubiennes, tant de tranquillité et une confiance si grande dans la modération de la Russie? Cela m'étonne, et me suggère des craintes dont je ne puis me défendre.*" De Tocqueville to Lamoricière (no date), in R. Pierre Marcel, *Essai Politique sur Alexis de Tocqueville* (Paris, 1910), p. 500.

Constantinople, but on Buda. Immediately before
the occupation, Lord Bloomfield had written to him
that the attention of the Russian Government was
"more particularly directed to Hungary and Croatia,
and to the proceedings of the Slavonic tribes at
Carlowitz[1]." That Palmerston took the same view
was manifest already before the end of 1848:

"There are some who imagine," he wrote, "that the
advance of that force into those provinces is not wholly
unconnected with the events which have been passing
in Hungary, and that the Emperor has contemplated the
possibility of his being asked by the Austrian Government to assist in restoring order at Pest[2]."

Three days afterwards, he repeated the same idea;
in the latter despatch he asserts that a lengthy
occupation of the Principalities was not to be expected, for the Austrian Government had just been
successful at Vienna, and therefore had nothing
serious to apprehend either from the revolt at home
or from the "civil dissensions" in Hungary[3].

At the end of January, the intention of the Russian
General Lüders to use Wallachia as a stepping-stone
from Russia to Transylvania was known to Canning;
and in February that intention was carried out.

"It seems evident," wrote Palmerston on April 6th,
"that the occupation of the Principalities by Russian
troops, and the progressive increase in the number of
those troops, are measures which have been adopted

[1] Bloomfield to Palmerston, June 6th, 1848.
[2] Palmerston to Canning, Nov. 7th, 1848.
[3] Palmerston to Canning, Nov. 10th, 1848.

nearly as much with the view of enabling Russia to afford
military assistance to Austria in Hungary and Transylvania, as with reference to events which have happened
in the Principalities themselves; and if this is so it follows
that it cannot be expected that the Russians should
evacuate the Turkish provinces until the Civil War in
Hungary shall have been brought to a successful termination by the Austrians[1]."

The last phrase of this despatch is especially note-
worthy; it implies a quiet acquiescence in the task
which the Russians had set for themselves in the
occupation of the Principalities. It was, doubtless,
very wrong of them to use Turkish territory for such
purposes; but Palmerston would have been the last
to object to anything, even from St Petersburg,
tending to restore to the Viennese Government the
revolted eastern half of its lands. He wrote again,
a month later:

I always thought that one of the main motives for the
Russian occupation of the Danube provinces was a desire
to be ready to assist Austria in Hungary in case of need,
and this seems now to have been the case. How far it
may be wise for Austria, or how far it may answer her
ends in the long run, thus to have recourse to a Russian
army to coerce her own subjects, time will show: but
certainly one should think that she would have done
better to have tried all means of conciliation before she
had recourse to such foreign aid. It is possible, too, that
Russia may not find her account in this intervention to
the extent that she imagines; and, when so many of her
troops are gone abroad, she may find work start up for
them at home. However, we do not mean to meddle with

[1] Palmerston to Canning, April 6th, 1849.

the matter in the way of protest, or in any other manner. We of course attach great importance to the maintenance of the Austrian Empire as an essential element, and a most valuable one, in the balance of power, and we should deeply regret anything which should cripple Austria or impair her future independence[1].

Nor did Palmerston greatly fear the permanent acquiescence of Austria in Russian preponderance on the Lower Danube. On March 20th he wrote on the subject to Ponsonby:

I have to instruct Your Excellency to take an opportunity of drawing the attention of the Austrian Government to the proof which the recent entrance of Russian troops from Wallachia into Transylvania has afforded of the great importance which would attach to the Danube Principalities, if in the possession of Russia, as strategic points from whence the Austrian Empire might be threatened and attacked. The Austrian Government may at the present moment think only of the advantages which it has derived from the entrance of a friendly military force into an Austrian Province which is in a state of revolt, but the Austrian Government is too sagacious not to look further into futurity, and not to see that if a strong Power like Russia was to be in possession of the Principalities, instead of their being held by a weak Power like Turkey, the security of the Austrian Empire from attack on its eastern frontier would be very sensibly diminished[2].

From the time of the first Russian incursion into Transylvania the question of the violation of Turkish

[1] Palmerston to Canning, May 7th, 1849, quoted in Lane-Poole, vol. II. pp. 188–9.

[2] Palmerston to Ponsonby, March 20th, 1849.

neutrality by the belligerents became of increasing importance. Already on February 14th, Sir Stratford Canning had written that the Porte had been

called upon to take a decision with respect to any Hungarians or other Austrian subjects who, in the course of their military operations in Transylvania may, from choice or necessity, cross the frontier into Moldavia or Wallachia....The imperial troops are to be received as friends, the Hungarians and other subjects in revolt to be disarmed, and, without being given up, to be prevented from doing further injury to the Austrian Government[1].

From that time to the very end, Palmerston sent despatch after despatch[2] to Constantinople, counselling the strictest neutrality (or approving of Canning's admonitions to that effect), and the avoidance of anything which might lead to war between Turkey and her two powerful neighbours: it would never do to have a war in the Near East with Austria and Russia fighting under the same flag. That was why he and Sir Stratford constantly warned the Porte not to increase the number of Turkish troops in the Principalities, but to have the bulk in reserve in Bulgaria; for the relations between the Russian and Turkish armies of occupation were exceedingly delicate, and a general war might easily result from a skirmish between outposts.

[1] Canning to Palmerston, Feb. 14th, 1848, *Correspondence*, No. 121.

[2] Palmerston to Canning: March 20th, June 26th, July 2nd, July 7th, July 26th, Aug. 27th. All of these are to be found in the Bluebook.

"The abstinent course," he writes, as a diplomatist and not as a declaimer, "is the more particularly prudent, because, while the sympathies of the Porte must obviously be on the side of the Hungarians, the chances of success are in favour of the Imperialists; and there would be reason to fear that any expression of the sentiments of the Turkish Government, while it would have no effect in turning the balance between the contending parties, would involve the Porte in after-difficulties, if the contest should lead to the result which there seems reason to anticipate[1]."

Palmerston in Downing Street had an easier task than Sir Stratford Canning at Therapia. On the one hand there was always the danger that the Divan would be frightened by the Russian agents into compliance with demands which must have made Turkey an active participant in the warfare in Hungary. The Russian diplomatists at Constantinople were only less clever than Canning himself, and their logic had a perpetual tendency to savour of the camp rather than of the schools. If this was true of Titoff, the Russian minister at the Porte, it was still more so of General Grabbe, aide-de-camp of the Czar, who arrived, in April 1849, on the special mission of bullying the Turkish ministers until they should grant all that his imperial master demanded with respect to the Principalities. It was an open secret, also, that Russian intrigue and Russian

---

[1] Palmerston to Canning, July 26th, 1849. The despatch, in a mutilated form, is given in the Bluebook (No. 244); but not one word of the extract given above is there printed.

roubles were at work night and day striving to turn
out of office the two most powerful and most Liberal
of the Sultan's advisers, Reshid Pasha, the Grand
Vizier, and Aali Pasha, the Foreign Secretary. The
Sultan himself was a Liberal, and ever inclined to lend
a friendly ear to the words of the English minister.
But he was, at the same time, the weakest of
monarchs. A large Russian army was already within
his frontiers, while England was distant by the
whole breadth of a continent; and Canning, throughout the summer of 1849, received no word from
Palmerston enabling him to promise Turkey the
material support of England in the event of a definite
rupture between Russia and the Porte. The outcome
of this was that, when the question of the Principalities
was settled, Russia, in spite of some slight concessions, carried most of her points[1]. Canning was
bitterly disappointed, and his despatches for once
sound a note of despair. Palmerston, on the contrary,
was singularly unmoved. He wrote to Constantinople, praising Canning for the amount he had
accomplished with the "limited diplomatic means"
at his disposal, and fully recognised the objectionable
points in the *Acte* agreed upon by Russia and Turkey.
Had the British Government advised the Porte to
refuse all the Russian demands, and promised to bear
it "harmless through its refusal," the Porte would
doubtless have made good its stand against those
demands. "But many circumstances and various
considerations interfered to prevent Her Majesty's

[1] Canning to Palmerston, April 28th, 1849.

Government from taking such a course[1]." Unquestionably, one of the chief of those various considerations was the desire to see the Hungarians restored to their proper allegiance.

On the other hand, during the spring and summer of 1849 there was always the danger that Russian insolence would outstrip itself, and drive the Turks into the arms of the Hungarians. Practically the whole population of the Turkish Empire, Christians as well as Mahometans, were ardently pro-Magyar. Certainly, the two great Pashas, Reshid and Aali (the latter especially), were frankly on that side; as was also the Sultan, when not immediately under the influence or fear of the Russian agents. This sympathy of the Turks for the Hungarians had, of course, a large admixture of egoism in it. A constitutional and independent Hungary (which perhaps meant also a constitutional and independent Poland) the chief maxim of whose foreign policy would be resistance to Russian aggrandisement towards the south-west, was a decidedly more desirable neighbour than that Austrian Empire which seemed destined to be henceforth the helpmeet of Russia, and the agent of which at Constantinople, Baron Stürmer, was simply the *alter ego* of Titoff[2].

Kossuth had, from the very first, recognised the

---

[1] Palmerston to Canning, June 1st, 1849.

[2] Canning to Palmerston, July 5th, 1849. See also Teleki's letters to Pulszky at the end of the second volume of the latter's autobiography; and Rosen, *Geschichte der Türkei vom Siege der Reform im Jahre 1826 bis zum Pariser Traktat 1856*, vol. II. p. 112, quoted in Alter, p. 126.

importance of Turkey as a potential ally of the Hungarians. The goodwill of the Porte it was all the more necessary to obtain, since Kossuth, no less than Palmerston, perceived what was the chief aim of the Russian occupation of the Danubian Principalities. So early as July 15th, 1848, Count Fedor Karacsay had received instructions for a mission to the Pasha of Belgrade, the Government of Servia, the Governor of Bosnia, and, if need be, to the Porte itself. Whether the mission was ever carried out or not is very doubtful[1]. At all events, after the Russian incursion

[1] Eduard von Wertheimer, *Graf Julius Andrássy, sein Leben und seine Zeit* (3 vols., Stuttgart, 1910–13), vol. I. pp. 20 *et seq*. The above sketch of Hungarian diplomacy at the Porte rests mainly on the second chapter of this work. Alter (pp. 127–8) says that Karacsay's mission was accomplished: "Karacsay did not reach Constantinople till the end of September in order to present himself to Reshid Pasha as the envoy of Hungary. But it was not to be his fate to achieve any success. England, whose ambassador, Sir Stratford Canning exercised a preponderant influence over the Porte, was in this year anxiously intent upon keeping the East free from any contact with the Revolution, and had to regard it as her chief task to restrain the Grand Vizier, who was far too much under the influence of the Polish Emigrants, from rash steps which might easily be followed by the most difficult complications. In these circumstances, it may be conjectured that Sir Stratford Canning played the protector of the 'wild diplomacy' at Constantinople chiefly with the view of keeping in close touch with the Hungarians in especial, in order to be precisely informed as to their plans, and to be able to intervene, should Reshid Pasha appear ready to give way to their insinuations. Count Karacsay, to whom at first Reshid Pasha had shown himself very well intentioned, soon found himself restricted to the *rôle* of a 'postmaster' of the Hungarian Government; he was not able to maintain the official relations with Reshid Pasha, notwithstanding the undiminished friendliness to the Hungarians maintained by the latter. Karacsay had thence-

into Transylvania, either towards the end of March
or the beginning of April, 1849, Baron Ludwig
Splényi was sent as ambassador to the Porte[1]. He
had before this been ambassador at Turin; but, after
Custozza, his continued stay in that capital was use-
less, and fraught with danger both for himself and
for the monarch to whom he was accredited. He
perceived that Sir Stratford Canning's sympathies
were with the Hungarians, and counselled Kossuth
to win over Palmerston through the English ambassador at Constantinople. With him was associated a
Major Browne[2]. In the course of April, the young

forth no other task than that of negotiating the epistolary
correspondence between the Hungarian Government and
foreign countries which had to be carried on via Constantinople,
and even to this modest activity the first march of the
Russians into Transylvania in February, 1849, put an end.
Thanks to the retarding influence of Sir Stratford Canning,
the friendliness of the Porte towards Hungary did not go so
far as to involve England in any difficulties with Russia on
behalf of Hungary, while Russia, by the helpful intervention
in favour of the Corps Pucher, openly placed herself on the
side of Austria. Only a single day after the news of the entry
of the Russians into Transylvania Karacsay was advised by the
Porte to make himself scarce." Alter's sole authorities are three
despatches of Canning to Palmerston, and one of Palmerston
to Canning. None of these despatches is to be found either
in the Bluebook or the F. O. records in Chancery Lane.

[1] Reiner, in his articles on "Hungarian Diplomacy at Constantinople" in the *Neue Freie Presse* (Feb. 21st, 22nd and 26th,
1890), speaks of Splényi as Palmerston's agent. This is of
course absurd. Wertheimer notes the mistake.

[2] Canning announced Major Browne's arrival to Palmerston
on May 19th, 1849. In a postscript added to that despatch on
May 25th, he stated that the Major was to have an interview
with some one appointed by the Porte to see him. At the same
time, the arrival of Splényi as Browne's secretary was announced.

Count Julius Andrássy was named ambassador to the Sultan. The journey from Hungary to Constantinople was a long and dangerous affair for a Hungarian agent in the early summer of 1849, and the Count did not reach his destination until towards the end of June. Although the Hungarians in Constantinople observed the greatest secrecy, the Austrian and Russian diplomats in that city knew of their activities[1], and of course directed the Porte to break off all intercourse with such "agitators," and, indeed, to expel them beyond the Turkish frontiers. The Turks, as usual, sought to navigate between Scylla and Charybdis.

"Influenced alike by their interests and their fears," wrote Canning, "the Turkish ministers continue to steer a middle course, as well as they can. They have engaged Baron Splényi, a Hungarian agent, to withdraw, at the requisition of the Russian and Austrian legations, and they have consented with reluctance to announce publicly his departure, as an act of expulsion from the country, though in reality he was neither ordered away nor allowed to go without marks of sympathy from the Porte. Two other knowing, though unrecognised, agents from the Hungarian Government—a Major Browne and Count Andrássy—are allowed to remain here and to communicate secretly with persons in the employment of the Porte. If I am rightly informed, even the purchase of firearms for exportation to Hungary is not interdicted,

---

[1] Stürmer announced Andrássy's arrival in a despatch to Schwarzenberg, dated July 4th, Wertheimer, *loc. cit.* The Hungarian told the Porte in so many words that he would not accede to a request for his departure, especially if it emanated from the Austrian Internuncio.

and the means of conveying them to that country are
already provided by merchants engaged in trading to
the Danube[1]."

Andrássy, no less than Splényi, knew that Canning
was friendly to the Hungarians, and accordingly
called upon him; but the ambassador, though
receiving Andrássy and his companions with civility,
told them that he could not hold any intercourse
with them except as private individuals[2]. To have
dealings with the Hungarians at Constantinople was
indeed to play with fire, for Andrássy's object was to
bring about a collision between the Turkish and
Russian troops in the Principalities, and so to precipitate that general European conflict from behind the
smoke of which the Magyars were to emerge into
freedom. Whatever Canning's sentiments on the
matter might have been—and he would most
assuredly have faced calmly a general war on the
question of the Principalities—he was resolved
loyally to serve his chief[3]. Thus, day after day he
offered the invariable advice—Palmerston's advice—
to his Turkish friends: preserve your neutrality. In
Hungary itself, this advice from England was seen

[1] Canning to Palmerston, July 5th, 1849.
[2] Canning to Palmerston, Aug. 4th, 1849.
[3] As already mentioned, Kasimir Batthyányi believed that
the plan of a Balkan Confederation which should include
Hungary in a subordinate position was Canning's. This is not
at all improbable; but there is nothing on the subject in his
official despatches to Palmerston, or in the private letters
preserved at the Public Record Office. What he thought about
the reduction of Hungary by Russian arms is seen in a despatch
of his, dated Aug. 25th, 1849.

to mean, in fact, that the Russians might continue to use the Principalities as the stepping-stone to Transylvania, while the Hungarians could hope for nothing from the Balkans. Is it true, wrote Kasimir Batthyányi to Pulszky, that, although Canning himself is favourable to us, he has received despatches from home not favourable to Hungary[1]? It was true; but those despatches contained outwardly no single word which could be characterised as inimical to the Magyar cause.

Canning, however, was able to render one not inconsiderable service to his friends. By sea, the Austrians were, practically, powerless; and this, in view of the close relations which existed between Turin and Pest, meant that the Adriatic was liable to be used as a highway of revolution. In February 1849, therefore, two Austrian officers arrived at Constantinople for the purchase of vessels of war from the Sultan, who, in his desire to placate his neighbours of Vienna and St Petersburg, showed himself at first not unfavourable to their proposal—and even entertained the idea of a gift of several vessels from the Egyptian fleet. The negotiations were carried on for some weeks; but ultimately the emphatic protests of the English, French and Sardinian representatives were successful, and the Austrians relinquished the idea[2].

[1] Teleki to Pulszky, June 21st and July 14th, 1849.
[2] Series of despatches, Canning to Palmerston, from Feb. 4th to March 14th, 1849; and the Note of the Sardinian Foreign Minister De Ferrari to the French and English Governments (in a despatch of Abercromby to Palmerston, March 12th, 1849).

Palmerston's speeches in the House of Commons fully bear out what has been said concerning his policy, and the illustrations already cited from his diplomatic correspondence. On May 11th, 1849, Pulszky's friend Bernal Osborne asked whether the Cabinet had any intention of offering their mediation "between the Emperor of Austria and the victorious people of Hungary"? Palmerston replied that the Government "had taken steps to offer their mediation between Austria and Hungary, and the Austrian Government had intimated no desire for such mediation[1]." These few unvarnished words of response made it painfully clear to all friends of Hungary in the West, that even after the Russian intervention had been announced—Palmerston had that day received a despatch from Vienna on the subject—the policy of the Government would be unchanged: for them there still existed no "Government of Hungary," and they would not arrogate to themselves any right of interfering in what was plainly a Viennese family affair. But the friends of Hungary were now legion, and the Russian intervention had created a profounder stir than anything that had

[1] Hansard, cv. p. 326: "In the earlier part of the year Lord Palmerston had vainly attempted to mediate between the contending parties in Hungary, so as to avert the Russian intervention." Ashley, vol. ii. p. 104. This is the reverse of true. The Radicals in the country murmured that, although the Foreign Secretary might with truth say that the Austrians had no wish for his mediation, he was silent about the Hungarians, who did "earnestly desire such mediation, and had been coldly repulsed." See the pamphlet of the indignant Washington Wilks, *Palmerston in Three Epochs* (London, 1854).

happened since the outbreak of the war. In addition
to this, the journalistic campaign of Pulszky and his
friends was beginning to tell in every corner of the
kingdom. As July passed away and the Magyars
still, with real heroism and some success, contended
against the Fieldmarshals of two Empires, the
genuine British hatred towards the unrepentant
successors of the Holy Alliance, indignation at the
atrocities daily reported, and the customary sympathy with the little battalions, asserted themselves.
Industrial centres without a grain of romance in them,
fashionable watering-places and remote hamlets in
the Highlands, were at one in their enthusiasm for
the revolution and their detestation of the perjured
Habsburgs. Government woke up and found the
land Magyar. Palmerston's popularity was gravely
menaced, and the only Radical who had ever held a
Foreign portfolio was accused of covenanting away
the liberties of Europe to the reactionaries of the
Northern Courts. "Saul did not stone Stephen,
but Stephen's murderers laid down their clothes at
Saul's feet," wrote one correspondent towards the
end of July. That Palmerston's popularity did not
suffer more was due to the readiness of the public to
believe in the incorrigible timidity of his colleagues,
and the insidious manœuvres of the German camarilla at St James'. "Rumour says that you are
impeded by your colleagues," continues the correspondent just quoted. "Whether or not, would to God
that we had a Cabinet that represented England!"
Another correspondent was still more outspoken:

When this Power, incompetent in itself to perpetuate the spirit of absolutism, calls on its remote archetype for help, it is time that we forego our German sympathies and cousinage, and resume, with the memory of Lord Chatham, that "English sentiment" which deprecated the ruinous practice of subsidizing and amalgamating with foreigners[1].

And, on July 26th, Lord Beaumont presented in the Upper House a petition from the City of London itself, praying for the immediate recognition of the existence, *de facto*, of the kingdom of Hungary, for reasons of justice, policy, commerce and humanity[2]. Palmerston, like Henry VIII, kept a perpetual finger on the public pulse, and took his measures according to the registration. His speech on July 21st, in the full-dress debate on the Russian intervention, is in reality a much finer piece of artistry than the more celebrated *Civis Romanus* speech of eleven months later, and, since its aim was to restore the wavering Liberals to their allegiance, it was equally successful;

"this speech made him in a few days," said Bunsen, "the idol of the Radicals in England, and the most popular and most powerful Minister in Europe."

"The House," he said, "will not expect me to follow those who have spoken to-day by endeavouring to pass judgment either way between the Austrian Government and the Hungarian nation. I say the Hungarian nation, because, in spite of what has fallen from the noble Lord, the Member for Tyrone[3], I do believe from the informa-

---

[1] *Liverpool Mercury*, July 24th, 1849.
[2] Hansard, cvii. p. 962.
[3] Lord Claud Hamilton, who had just sat down.

tion I have received—and I do not pretend I may not be mistaken—but I firmly believe that in this war between Austria and Hungary, there are enlisted on the side of Hungary the hearts and the souls of the whole people of that country. I believe that the other races distinct from the Magyars have forgotten the former feuds that existed between them and the Magyar population, and that the greater portion of the people have engaged in what they consider a great national contest....

"I take the question that is now to be fought for on the plains of Hungary to be this—whether Hungary shall continue to maintain its separate nationality as a distinct kingdom, and with a constitution of its own; or whether it is to be incorporated more or less in the aggregate constitution that is to be given to the Austrian Empire? It is a most painful sight to see such forces as are now arrayed against Hungary proceeding to a war fraught with such tremendous consequences on a question that it might have been hoped would be settled peacefully. It is of the utmost importance to Europe that Austria should remain great and powerful; but it is impossible to disguise from ourselves that, if the war is to be fought out, Austria must thereby be weakened; because, on the one hand, if the Hungarians should be successful, and their success should end in the entire separation of Hungary from Austria, it will be impossible not to see that this will be such a dismemberment of the Austrian Empire as will prevent Austria from continuing to occupy the great position she has hitherto held among European Powers. If, on the other hand, the war being fought out to the uttermost, Hungary should by superior forces be entirely crushed, Austria in that battle will have crushed her own right arm. Every field that is laid waste, is an Austrian resource destroyed, every man that perishes upon the field among the Hungarian ranks, is an Austrian soldier deducted from the defensive forces of the Empire...

"It is, I say, devoutly to be wished that this great contest may be brought to a termination by some amicable arrangement between the contending parties, which shall on the one hand satisfy the national feeling of the Hungarians, and on the other hand not leave to Austria another and a larger Poland within her Empire. Her Majesty's Government have not, in the present state of the matter, thought that any opportunity has as yet presented itself that would enable them, with any prospect of advantage, to make any official communication of those opinions which they entertain on this subject. I say official, as contradistinguished from opinions expressed in a more private and confidential manner; but, undoubtedly, if any occasion were to occur that should lead them to think the expression of such opinions would tend to a favourable result, it would be the duty of the Government not to let such an opportunity pass by[1]."

He had said kind things of the Hungarians, and other speakers were saying kind things of the Hungarians and bitter things of the Austrians on a hundred platforms up and down the country—but there was to be no slightest change in his foreign policy. He could truthfully say that there were no official papers, because there had been no protest on

[1] Hansard, CVII. pp. 786–817. Bernal Osborne, seconded by Monckton Milnes, moved that copies of papers respecting the Russian invasion of Hungary and of "any communications which have passed involving naval or military aid or interference on the part of this country" be laid before the House. The portion of the speech dealing with the importance of Austria to the Balance of Power has already been quoted. Palmerston spoke seventh in the debate. In the course of the speech he stated that there were no official papers to produce; in consequence of which Bernal Osborne finally withdrew his motion. The extracts given above are a small part only of the speech, and not the best part.

his part to St Petersburg, and because he would not
take cognisance of the Hungarian offers and appeals.
He could safely promise not to let an opportunity
of fruitful mediation pass by, because he knew that
the time for fruitful mediation had long gone by,
and that, probably, before a despatch could reach
Vienna "free and independent" Hungary would be
matter for diplomatic historians, but not for diplomatists, to wrangle over. On August 1st Parliament
was prorogued, and it did not meet again until
January 31st, 1850.

It has been asserted in various quarters that
Palmerston not only by his passive attitude throughout, but on one occasion at least actively, proved
himself the enemy of Hungarian independence.
According to this view, the French Cabinet asked
the Foreign Office whether they intended to take
diplomatic steps against the Russian intervention;
if this were the case, and such steps were of a friendly
nature, France was willing to associate herself with
England. To this question the French Foreign
Minister, Drouyn de Lhuys, received the reply that
England for the present did not feel herself called
upon to adopt any sort of position in the matter[1].

---

[1] Alter, p. 157. His authority ("official correspondence
between Palmerston and Lord Normanby, undated") I have
not been able to discover. Teleki believed the statement.
See his letter to Pulszky, dated June 30th, 1849. Alter, of
course, knew the contents of the letter; but his book claims
to be based on "new authorities," and he therefore documents
this portion of it with non-existent official despatches.

But for this answer of Palmerston's, we are told,
Hungary might have been saved. Such an assertion
displays woeful ignorance of French official circles in
the summer months of 1849. If Palmerston, on general
grounds of good statesmanship, could not afford to
let the Magyars wrest their ancient freedom from
the only Government which had bombarded every
important city in its dominions, there were a dozen
immediate and special reasons why Louis Napoleon
should not do so. In his heart of hearts, he wished
to roll up the map of 1815; but this was only to
be done with the consent and cooperation of the
Northern Courts. The Czar must be made to see that
the Parisians had definitely done with barricades,
and would henceforth conduct their politics after a
more reasonable fashion; Schwarzenberg must be
set at rest respecting the imminent expedition to
Cività Vecchia. Madame de Tocqueville told Teleki
and Pulszky that Louis Napoleon had made only one
condition when her husband took over the Foreign
portfolio at the beginning of June: he was not to
interfere in the Roman expedition which had already
set out. De Tocqueville remembered the condition.
"I especially kept up friendly relations with Austria,"
he writes, "whose concurrence was necessary to us
in the Roman business[1]." During the autumn
months, the French agent Persigny was at work
stealthily among the German Courts, trying to
discover how these would receive the news of a
coup d'état beyond the Rhine which should beget an

[1] *Recollections*, p. 355.

Empire that was Napoleonic but not revolutionary[1].

On the very eve of the Russian invasion of Hungary, Nicholas declared that he would recognise the French Republic[2]; and they were not so simple at the Quai d'Orsay as to believe that this was a piece of sheer imperial benevolence. De Tocqueville's instructions to Lamoricière at St Petersburg on that invasion prove the contrary:

I need not tell you with what keen and melancholy interest we follow events in Hungary. Unfortunately, for the present, we can only take a passive part in this question. The letter and spirit of the treaties open out to us no right of intervention. Besides, our distance from the seat of war must impose upon us, in the present state of affairs and of those of Europe, a certain reserve. Since we are not able to speak or act to good purpose, it is due to our dignity not to display, in respect of this question, any sterile excitement or impotent good feeling. Our duty with regard to Hungarian events is to limit ourselves to carefully observing what happens, and seeking to discover what is likely to take place[3].

Even the optimist Teleki, who had once imagined that his word carried weight with Tocqueville, perceived at last that reaction reigned in Paris, and that nothing was to be expected from the French Government. His avowed readiness, for the rest, to put on

---

[1] Keller, *Le Général de Lamoricière* (2 vols., Paris, 1880), vol. II. p. 221. Persigny's presence was also known to the English representatives at Vienna and St Petersburg.

[2] Buchanan to Palmerston, May 8th, 1849.

[3] De Tocqueville to Lamoricière, undated. Printed in *Recollections*, p. 359.

the reddest of cockades if it would help the Hungarian cause, was not behaviour adapted to win over a country long since shamed of the February *journées*.

The rumour that France was willing to save the Hungarians from the hordes of Russia doubtless takes its origin from the proceedings in the French Chamber on May 12th. On that date, M. Flocon interpellated the Government on their intentions with respect to the Russian intervention in Hungary. The Chamber was in a democratic mood, and very suspicious of the reactionary policy of the President; but the elections were at hand, and its days were numbered. It would have been bad statesmanship to inflame the passions of the Assembly at the eleventh hour, and consequently Drouyn de Lhuys, the Foreign Minister, made an untruthful answer, which was prodigally garnished with circumstantial detail intended to give verisimilitude to the narrative:

As soon as the French Government received knowledge of the intention which the Russian Government appeared to have of intervening in the affairs of Hungary, it realised the gravity of such a step. It announced at St Petersburg, Berlin, Vienna and London that so serious a complication could not pass unnoticed, and that it awakened the lively solicitude of the French Government. France is setting to work by *diplomacy* to prevent an action calculated, I repeat, seriously to disturb the state of affairs in the Near East, in Germany and in every region of Europe.

In this respect the Cabinet has done all that a prudent Government should do; it has striven to hinder, by the way of diplomacy, an affair which appeared to it very regrettable.

You ask what it will do; it will persist in this course of action, and if it were forced to have recourse to measures other than those which it has employed thus far, it would consult the Assembly concerning its new resolutions.

But both to Normanby and Kisseleff, the English and Russian representatives at Paris, Drouyn de Lhuys explained away the last paragraph[1].

On May 22nd and 23rd the Cabinet was again attacked on its policy at Rome and in Hungary. Drouyn replied that he had already mentioned the Government's representations at St Petersburg, London, Berlin and Vienna. *" Si l'on veut autre chose, si l'on veut la guerre, qu'on en apporte la proposition à la tribune !"* Finally an order of the day was passed, so amended, and couched in such general terms, that it might mean anything. The Extreme Left asserted that its adoption was equivalent to giving *carte blanche* to Russia; the English Chargé d'Affaires, on the contrary, wrote to Palmerston that it was a nasty business, and smelt of powder[2]. Fortunately, he added, the Assembly was dying, and the elections were already being held.

How much importance was to be attached to what the French Minister said, and repeated, concerning

[1] Lord Normanby to Palmerston, May 13th and 15th, 1849. Drouyn's reply is translated from the report in the *Moniteur* of Sunday, May 15th.

[2] May 23rd, 1849. See also Irányi and Chassin, vol. II. pp. 465–70.

the representations at the various capitals, is best
learnt from the mouths of the French agents abroad:

"I learn from the French Chargé d'Affaires," wrote
Magenis at Vienna, "that he has not as yet received any
instructions from M. Drouyn de Lhuys to make any
representations to this Government on the subject of the
Russian intervention in Hungary. M. de Lacour appeared
to me not to attach much importance to the declaration
of the French Minister for Foreign Affairs in the Chamber
on that subject[1]."

Our agent at St Petersburg was still more explicit.
So far as he knew, the only despatch which had been
received at the French legation there was one
instructing the French Chargé d'Affaires to make
some general observations "on the importance of the
measure, should it really be adopted by Russia."
But there was

nothing in the communication which gave it the
character of a diplomatic step; and indeed M. Seniavine
—Count Nesselrode was with the Czar at Warsaw at the
time—has since remarked to me that M. Drouyn de
Lhuys would have been much embarrassed if he had been
called upon by the Assembly to produce the communications to which he referred.

It does not appear to me that much importance was
attached here to M. Drouyn de Lhuys' answer to M.
Flocon; and I have found those persons with whom I
have spoken on the subject ready to accept what had
passed in the debate on the expedition to Italy as a good
reason for the French Government endeavouring to prevent, by a few *phrases*, a discussion on the Hungarian

[1] Magenis to Palmerston, May 22nd, 1849.

question with the late Assembly on the eve of its dissolution; and, had the matter been looked at more
seriously by the Emperor and Count Nesselrode, I think
we should have heard of it by this time[1].

At Warsaw Colonel du Plat had a conversation on
the subject with the Russian Chancellor himself.
The Chancellor declared that he was "much astonished" at the statement that representations had
been made by the French Government against the
Russian intervention in Hungary:

"I know nothing about it," he added, "neither directly
nor indirectly, either from the French Chargé d'Affaires
at St Petersburg, or from the Russian Minister at Paris;
and I am not aware that the Austrian Government has
received any such representations[2]."

The new Chamber, apparently, needed less management, and Ministers could safely adhere to the truth.
There were still interpellations whereby Ledru-Rollin
and Teleki's other friends tried to force the Government into a war; but nothing came of it, and, when
eighty-five members of the Mountain signed a proposition to recognise the independence and nationality of Hungary, it was unanimously rejected by the
Commission de l'initiative parlementaire. De Tocqueville, the new Foreign Minister, was politeness itself
when Teleki called upon him, but would not, of
course, do anything[3].

---

[1] Buchanan to Palmerston, June 1st, 1849 (Confidential).

[2] Du Plat to Palmerston, June 15th, 1849.

[3] Teleki to Pulszky, June 25th–26th, July 8th, Aug. 13th.
Lord Normanby to Palmerston, Aug. 12th, 1849.

On the very day on which Parliament was prorogued, Palmerston sent off two despatches to Ponsonby. The first of these, written with characteristic care, and more than characteristically didactic, contained reflections on the awful character of a "conflict between an entire nation and the armies of two great empires," between an "organised and well-equipped" army of 150,000 Hungarians and the Austrian force, "acknowledged to be by itself unable to make head against the Hungarians"— together with the "whole disposable force of the Russian Empire." It admitted that the Imperialists surely must be the victors sooner or later, but admitted, also, the remote probability of the Hungarian resistance being so obstinate and so prolonged, that the Austrians might ultimately deem it better policy to grant their antagonists peace on their own terms:

In such a case the separation of Hungary from the Austrian Crown would so weaken the Austrian Empire as an element in the balance of power, as to produce very unfortunate effects upon the general interests of Europe; and for that reason, as well as from the sincere and long-standing regard which the British Government and Nation entertain for Austria, such a dismemberment of the Austrian Empire would be regarded by Her Majesty's Government as a great political calamity.

But, admitting the inevitable superiority of numbers, would Austria obtain any permanent advantage from an ascendancy obtained and continued by force? "The discontent of the heart will not be extinguished merely because the hand has been disarmed."

Hungary so subdued would be a veritable "political cancer, corroding the vital elements of that empire's existence." And what would be the price paid to that ally "by whose gigantic exertions alone " Austria could conquer? The British Government had a right to enquire whether any arrangements were being contemplated at variance with the letter or spirit of the Treaty of Vienna. But Great Britain wished earnestly for an arrangement between the combatants, made, on the one hand, with the good-will of the Hungarian people, and calculated to satisfy their national feelings; but which would, on the other hand, "maintain unimpaired the bond of union which has so long connected Hungary with the Austrian Crown." It is the old tale: bitter food for Austrian digestion, but no independent Hungary[1].

The second despatch of that day contained an offer of mediation:

If Your Excellency should at any time see a disposition on the part of the Austrian Government to enter into negotiations with the Hungarians, and if you should have reason to think that the friendly intervention of a third party might in any respect be acceptable to the Austrian Government, as removing difficulties of any kind, Your Excellency is authorised to give the Austrian Government to understand that H.M. Government would feel great pleasure in attending without the least delay to any intimation which they might receive of the wishes of the Austrian Government to that effect[2].

[1] Palmerston to Ponsonby, Aug. 1st, 1849, *Correspondence*, No. 254. The despatch was to be read to Schwarzenberg.
[2] Palmerston to Ponsonby, same date, *Correspondence*,

Palmerston must have known that, so late in the day, such an offer would be rejected, even if the Austrians and Queen Victoria had not already had enough of his mediation in Italy. And, indeed, a despatch of Ponsonby's was already on its way to England, stating that such a proceeding could but raise difficulties in the way of what might be attempted hereafter[1]. Schwarzenberg refused to accept a copy of the first of the two despatches, and would have nothing to say to the offer of mediation:

"I was well prepared for the reception that subject would meet with," wrote Ponsonby, "I have already told Your Lordship that I thought the time was still *to come*, when it could be hoped that the Austrian Government would listen to it. I can see no good," he continues, angrily but logically, "in continuing to urge on this Government things which it is determined not to do, for I see no means by which it can be forced to change its conduct."

Ponsonby was constrained to leave the copy on the Minister's table, and three weeks later it still remained unread. But Schwarzenberg—a "Palmerston in white"—was not less skilful than the British statesman in composing despatches innocent of the daintier diplomatic amenities; and on September 19th sent a reply in kind to Count Colloredo, the Austrian Minister in London:

No. 255; see also Blackwell to Lord Eddisbury, Oct. 5th, 1849. Ponsonby had told Blackwell that he had received instructions to employ the latter in negotiations with the Hungarians, if the Austrian Ministers were willing.

[1] Ponsonby to Palmerston, July 29th, 1849, *Correspondence*, No. 259.

Events have taken upon themselves to reply to these communications of the Principal Secretary of State of Her Britannic Majesty, better than I could have done. There is no cause for surprise if the results to which the Hungarian insurrection has led are different from those which Lord Palmerston had anticipated, inasmuch as, destitute of the necessary elements on which he could form a competent opinion on this matter, he was reduced to information such as that promulgated in England by the agents of the Hungarian insurrection, whose interest it was to represent the events of which their country was the theatre in the falsest light, and to give the colouring of a generous and heroic impulse to an attempt which the English law qualifies as high treason, and which it punishes without fail with death or transportation. The world is agitated by a spirit of general subversion. England herself is not exempt from the influence of this spirit; witness Canada, the Island of Cefalonia, and finally, unhappy Ireland. But wherever revolt breaks out within the vast limits of the British Empire, the English Government always knows how to maintain the authority of the law, were it even at the price of torrents of blood. It is not for us to blame her. Whatever may, moreover, be the opinion which we form as to the causes of these insurrectionary movements, as well as of the measures of repression employed by the British Government in order to stifle them, we consider it our duty to abstain from expressing that opinion, persuaded as we are that persons are apt to fall into gross errors, in making themselves judges of the often so complicated position of foreign countries. By this conduct we consider we have acquired the right to expect that Lord Palmerston will practise with respect to us a perfect reciprocity[1].

[1] Schwarzenberg to Colloredo, Sept. 26th, 1849, *Correspondence*, No. 326. Friedjung, vol. II. part I. p. 136. The French

On August 22nd the telegraphic report of Görgei's surrender reached England, and six days later Palmerston wrote to Vienna expressing satisfaction at the successful termination of the war:

"The eyes of all Europe," he continues, in his loftiest moral tone, "will of course now be directed to the proceedings of the Austrian Government in a matter which has excited so deep and general an interest; and H.M. Government would fail in the performance of their duty if they were not to instruct you to express the anxious hope which they feel, in common with the people of this country, that the Austrian Government would make a generous use of the successes which it has obtained, and that in the arrangements which may be made between the Emperor of Austria and the Hungarian nation, due regard will be had to the ancient constitutional rights of Hungary. A settlement founded on such a basis, with such improvements as the altered circumstances of the present time may require, will be the best security not only for the welfare and contentment of Hungary, but also for the future strength and prosperity of the Austrian Empire[1]."

Government was prevailed upon by Palmerston to express similar sentiments at Vienna. Palmerston to Normanby, Aug. 10th, 1849. The Canadian Rebellion was a source of great edification to the Austrians at that time. "The fire in his own house will in the future spoil Lord Firebrand's game of setting in flames the houses of his neighbours. The policy of the English Cabinet has been such as to oblige Europe to regard as a piece of good fortune for herself any evil fortune which may befal England." Leading Article of the official *Vienna Lloyd* of Aug. 11th.

[1] Palmerston to Ponsonby, Aug. 28th, 1849, *Correspondence*, No. 301. The French Government made similar representations, see Palmerston to Ponsonby, Aug. 31st, 1849.

At home, meanwhile, the newspapers were flooded with reports of the savage and degrading punishments which the conquerors were meting out to the conquered. The lost Magyar cause was gaining converts by thousands, and every post brought Palmerston a budget of memorials praying that the Queen and Government should do something for the Hungarians. The Foreign Secretary kept pace with his public, and the memorials were duly despatched to Vienna— for the conversion of the erring Ponsonby, apparently, since it could scarcely be expected that Schwarzenberg would read and profit by them. The Ambassador was also instructed to find out the truth about the alleged barbarities; the public flogging of ladies, the shooting of prisoners in cold blood and the hanging of priests for the mere expression of political opinions. His replies were always favourable to the Austrians, and usually betrayed both exasperation and scorn at Palmerston's faith in mere journalists[1]. Such of the series as were laid before the Houses of Parliament were drastically mutilated and softened down before they were considered meet for public perusal. The newspaper reporters, and not Ponsonby, won the day with Palmerston, as the following letter shows:

The Austrians are really the greatest brutes that ever called themselves by the undeserved name of civilised men. Their atrocities in Galicia, in Italy, in Hungary, in Transylvania, are only to be equalled by the proceedings of the negro race in Africa and Haiti. Their

[1] Palmerston to Ponsonby, Aug. 2nd, Sept. 22nd, Oct. 5th; Ponsonby to Palmerston, Aug. 7th, Oct. 2nd, Oct. 30th.

late exploit of flogging forty odd people, including two women at Milan, some of the victims being gentlemen, is really too blackguard and disgusting a proceeding. As to working upon their feelings of generosity and gentlemanlikeness, that is out of the question, because such feelings exist not in a set of officials who have been trained up in the school of Metternich, and the men in whose minds such inborn feelings have not been crushed by Court and office power, have been studiously excluded from public affairs, and can only blush in private for the disgrace which such things throw upon their country. But I do hope that *you* will not fail constantly to bear in mind the country and the Government which you represent, and that you will maintain the dignity and honour of England by expressing *openly* and *decidedly* the disgust which such proceedings excite in the public mind in this country; and that you will not allow the Austrians to imagine that the public opinion of England is to be gathered from articles put into the *Times* by Austrian agents in London, or from the purchased support of the *Chronicle*, or from the servile language of Tory lords and ladies in London, or from the courtly notions of royal dukes and duchesses.... The rulers of Austria (I call them not statesmen or stateswomen) have now brought their country to this remarkable condition, that the Emperor holds his various territories at the goodwill and pleasure of three external Powers. He holds Italy just as long as, and no longer than, France chooses to let him have it. The first quarrel between Austria and France will drive the Austrians out of Lombardy and Venice. He holds Hungary and Galicia just as long as, and no longer than, Russia chooses to let him have them. The first quarrel with Russia will detach those countries from the Austrian Crown. He holds his German provinces by a tenure dependent, in a great degree, upon feelings and opinions which it will be very difficult for him and his ministers either to combine or to stand out against. The remedy against these various dangers, which are rapidly undermining the Austrian Empire, would be generous conciliation; but, instead of that, the Austrian Government know no method of administration but what consists in flogging, imprisoning and shooting. "The Austrians know no argument but force!"[1]

During the course of the war, a considerable number of English subjects incurred the wrath of the Austrian Government for real or alleged implication with the Revolution. The woes and injuries of the itinerant British citizen ever roused the fighting spirit in Palmerston, and some of the sharpest words that ever passed between the two Governments concerned themselves only indirectly with foreign policy properly so-called. Palmerston and Ponsonby were still bandying words with each other about the mistakes of English journalists and the misdeeds of Austrian officials, when there occurred an event so serious that their correspondence was suddenly diverted into an altogether different channel, and for several days it seemed not improbable that there would soon be no longer any English Ambassador at Vienna. The two Imperial Courts had demanded the extradition of the Hungarian and Polish refugees in Turkey.

Within a few days of Görgei's surrender, about 5000 Hungarians and Poles had sought safety by crossing the Danube into Turkish territory. Among

---

[1] Ashley, vol. II. pp. 105–7. Alter speaks as though this private letter had been an official despatch.

these refugees were Kossuth, five Cabinet Ministers, and some of the chief leaders of the late Hungarian army. Of the Poles, the chief were the old Napoleonic campaigner Dembinski, Bem, most brilliant of all Sarmatian warriors, Count Ladislaus Zamoyski, who had acquired French nationality, and General Wyzocki. It was not for a moment to be hoped that the imperial hunt would allow much of the most desirable quarry to escape; that Austria would relinquish without an effort the man "who was the Hungarian Revolution"; or that the Czar would calmly see so many seeds of revolt scattered without let or hindrance over the face of Europe. Schwarzenberg and Nesselrode were able to base their demands of extradition upon certain definite treaty stipulations; applying to Austrian subjects the Treaties of Belgrade (Art. XVIII) and Passarowitz (Art. XIV), and to Russian subjects the Treaty of Kainardji (Art. II). The friends of humanity and Turkish independence were quick to see the legal flaws in the Austrian and Russian demands; for the Austrian treaties make no mention whatever of mutual surrender of refugees, while the treaty with Russia left it optional for each party either to deliver up refugees or to expel them from its territory[1]. The two first-mentioned treaties, certainly, imposed the obligation of punishing "*sujets rebelles et mécontents*" upon both contracting parties. The meaning and extent of this

[1] Palmerston to Canning, Oct. 6th, 1849, *Correspondence respecting Refugees from Hungary within the Turkish Dominions* (presented to both Houses of Parliament by Command of Her Majesty, Feb. 28th, 1851), No. 18.

stipulation were the real crux. The statesmen of Turkey and the Western Powers agreed that the clauses in question applied to offenders in time of peace, but contended that they could not be stretched to include a whole nation become fugitive because it had been fighting for its constitutional rights. All the chanceries, however, knew perfectly well that the clumsy official French of a hundred years and more ago would not decide the fate of Kossuth and his companions; this would be decided by the amount of support which the Sultan could expect from his distant friends at London and Paris. This, again, would depend largely on the opinions entertained by the English and French representatives on the spot. Sir Stratford Canning and his French colleague— "*bien endoctriné par Sir Stratford*"—never hesitated from the first; for them it was not a question of solving the grammatical ambiguities of a forgotten generation, but a question of living interests, of the maintenance of the Balance of Power. Enough has already been said of what Sir Stratford Canning thought of St Petersburg diplomacy, and of the goal of that diplomacy. The despatch in which he announces the demands of the Russian and Austrian agents for extradition of the whole number of refugees, and the decision of the Porte, if those demands were pressed and reiterated, to appeal ultimately to the leading Powers, contains also his view of what lay behind Világos:

On the whole it is but reasonable to expect that the present successes will be used to promote the great

objects of Russian policy throughout the East, and that
endeavours will be made under the impressions created
by victory to draw the Turkish Government into a more
complete subserviency to the political views of that
Power. How far the Cabinet of Vienna may be disposed
or obliged to act as an auxiliary to Russia in carrying
out these views, whether, as some believe, the question
of extradition has been raised for sinister purposes, and
what measures of intimidation or aggression may follow
upon the Porte's continued refusal to give up the refugees,
the course of events will best serve to show. But I should
fail in my duty if I did not again solicit Your Lordship's
attention pointedly to this subject, and declare my conviction that, with every exertion on the part of Her
Majesty's Government and Embassy, it will henceforward
be more difficult than ever to keep the Sultan and his
Ministers in that course of policy which they have lately
pursued with tolerable pretensions to steadiness in their
way; and further, that, without stronger guarantees than
any I have heard of as already existing, it will hardly be safe
to overlook the inducements which, naturally enough in
the present state of Europe, may prevail with the Russian
Cabinet to bring the Porte into its views by force, if
persuasion fails, even in defiance of public opinion
elsewhere[1].

It has already been said also that Canning regarded
the Russian incursion into Hungary as a milestone
on the road from St Petersburg to Constantinople;
in August 1849 that milestone was safely passed, and
the next along the route was the affair of the refugees.
Here, at least, the Russians should find a check.

[1] Canning to Palmerston, Sept. 3rd, 1849. *Refugees*, No. 3.
But the whole of the extract given above is there omitted.

"Is Kossuth's skin worth a European war?" asked de Tocqueville, when he heard of the demand for extradition. "Perhaps not," Canning would have replied; "but, my friend, this is a question, not of Kossuth's skin, but of the balance of power." Already on August 30th, the Council of the Porte decided that they could not without dishonour give up the refugees, though the bitterness of refusal was to be softened down by a skilful use of those blandishments and that sweet reasonableness which still characterises Ottoman diplomacy *vis-à-vis* of its Christian neighbours. And, in fact, the Turkish reply to Titoff's note contained so much that was blandishment, and so little that was refusal, that Canning, to whom, of course, it was shown before being sent off, amended it drastically[1]. The Sultan undertook to perform all that could be claimed on the score of friendship and neighbourliness; the refugees should be removed from the frontier and they should be prevented from hatching plots against the two Emperors on Turkish soil. Meanwhile, in Russia the Government had divined that their demands might not receive that immediate and unqualified compliance which they desired—they knew Canning of old—and had recourse to the step which they were wont to take at such conjunctures. They sent Prince Michael Radzivil—himself of Polish extraction, and inspired with the renegade's zeal against his former

[1] Canning to Palmerston, Sept. 3rd, 1849. "Most Confidential," and of course not printed in the Whitebook on the Refugees.

brethren—with an autograph letter from the Czar to the Sultan, peremptorily demanding the extradition of the refugees. When the letter was delivered to the Sultan, its bearer hinted plainly enough that 50,000 Russians were ready to march into Turkey at a word from the Czar[1]. The letter was supplemented by Nesselrode's equally imperative instructions to Titoff: what Russia expected from the Porte was not a thesis in false philanthropy, but a categorical "yes" or "no"! The future relations of the two empires would, Nesselrode declared, depend on the purport of this answer. As though this were not enough, Titoff and Stürmer went yet a step further, and declared that the escape of a single refugee would be regarded by their masters as a declaration of war.

The steamer bearing Radzivil had arrived in the Bosphorus in the early hours of September 4th, and Canning, on hearing of the Prince's mission, saw at once how uncertain the future was. When it came to a real trial of strength between Russia and the Porte, the latter was not likely to hold its ground for long. Already before the Czar's letter had been handed in, the Porte had shown its willingness to yield much more than Canning could honestly counsel, and now Radzivil's advent might easily frustrate all his endeavours in the direction of honour and independence. The despatch announcing the momentous event of September 4th, and its possible

[1] Andrássy to Kossuth, Sept. 11th, 1849, in Wertheimer, *op. cit.* p. 42.

consequences, closes on the old note: "The resource of an appeal to Europe may sustain its courage for the present; but the ultimate issue will naturally depend upon the prospect of support from England and France[1]." In a private letter to Palmerston, of the same date, Canning was still more urgent: "I hope you will feel yourself at liberty to support us, and that speedily." For a time, everything was doubtful, and then the Porte took a step characteristically Turkish: on September 10th it decided to say neither "yes" nor "no," but to make a direct representation to the Czar at Warsaw, whose heart might perhaps prove not to be adamant like that of his stewards, while, at any rate, time would be gained. Fuad Effendi, one of the cleverest of Turkish diplomats, and *persona grata* at St Petersburg, was entrusted with this mission, and was to be the bearer of the Sultan's autograph reply to the letter brought by Prince Radzivil. His departure took place in the greatest secrecy, and he was over the Russian frontier before Stürmer and Titoff knew that he had been selected for the mission. When they were aware of the fact, on September 15th, they threatened to suspend diplomatic relations from the next day, unless they received a categorical and satisfactory answer to their demands. Three empires were on the

---

[1] Canning to Palmerston, Sept. 5th, 1849. *Refugees*, No. 5. (Extract only.) Many of the omissions in the Whitebook serve to hide the intimacy of Canning's relations with Aali and Reshid. Not a note was sent, not a Conference held, during the crisis, in which, or at which, the Turks did not write or say what Canning told them.

brink of war; but Canning was firm in his advice.
He was emboldened by the suspicion that Titoff and
the Internuncio were acting without instructions.

Nevertheless, "it is at all events manifest," he wrote,
"that the demand of the allied Courts, whatever may be
its real motive, or eventual limitation, is too seriously
entertained to warrant any line of conduct in resistance
to it, not formed in contemplation of the worst."

In face of the new danger the Council was again
divided, and that night Aali, the Foreign Minister,
sent Canning and General Aupick a paper containing
half-a-dozen questions. The independence of the
Ottoman Empire depended upon the answer given
to the fourth of those questions. If Russia were to
declare war, asked Aali, could the Porte count upon
the effective cooperation—*un concours efficace*—of
England and France? "It is plainly to be presumed,"
answered Canning and Aupick, "that the two Governments... would not leave the Porte without support,
should it be necessary[1]." Early on the 16th, the
Sultan got the answers, and Canning was able to
write home that the Porte intended to adhere to its
previous intention[2]. On the next day, the Austrian

[1] Canning to Palmerston, Sept. 16th, 1849, *Refugees*, No. 11.
[2] Canning to Palmerston, Sept. 16th, 1849, *Refugees*, No. 12;
and Edmond Bapst, *L'Empereur Nicholas I*er *et la deuxième
République française* (Paris, 1898; privately printed), pp. 87 ff.
Bapst's in French, and Lane-Poole's in English, *Life of Stratford Canning*, vol. II, are the only two accounts of the Affair
of the Refugees which can be trusted. Alter apparently knew
neither, and his narrative certainly does not improve upon
them.

and Russian embassies hauled down their flags, and Radzivil sailed northwards with his purpose unaccomplished, but bearing a letter which contained what was neither categorical nor satisfactory. Canning had triumphed so far; but the drama was merely at the end of the first act.

"If the Porte be left in this strait to its own resources," he wrote, "there will be a complete and perhaps an unavoidable breakdown of all that it has been hitherto the object of British policy to maintain, beyond its ordinary relations, with this Empire[1]."

The same day he wrote to Vice-Admiral Sir William Parker, Commander of the Mediterranean fleet, apprising the sailor of what was happening at Constantinople, and requesting that "a part at least of Her Majesty's Mediterranean squadron might be available for any purposes of demonstration in the Archipelago[2]." After that, there was nothing to do save to await the arrival of messengers from Downing Street, and encourage the Porte to hold fast to the decision it had so courageously taken. On October 3rd arrived the *Odin* frigate, with despatches from Parker, who intended to cruise between the Ionian waters and Athens until he should hear more from the Admiralty—for he too, of course, was acting without instructions from home. The Turks were much gratified by the news, unofficial though it was, and Canning must have been not a little cheered at so

[1] Canning to Palmerston, Sept. 17th, 1849, *Refugees*, No. 13.
[2] Canning to Sir William Parker, Sept. 17th, 1849, *Refugees*, No. 14.

slight an incident; anything which gave heart to the Turks was welcome to him just then. It was about this time that he heard of the attempt to convert the refugees at Widdin to Islamism, and of the dissatisfaction which this attempt had raised; the way of honour did not lie in that direction, and Canning told the Turkish Ministers, with characteristic candour, what he thought about it[1].

The extremely serious nature of affairs on the Bosphorus, the rupture of diplomatic relations and the unceremonious departure of Prince Radzivil, were known in London in the closing days of September. Parliament was not sitting, and most people were out of town at the time. Before the Cabinet had an opportunity of meeting, Palmerston personally decided to support the Sultan. On September 29th, he wrote a private letter to the Ambassador at Paris:

I received yesterday afternoon, at Brocket, by a letter from Drouyn de Lhuys, the telegraphic message announcing the breaking off of diplomatic relations by the Austrian and Russian Ministers at Constantinople. I am unable at present to send you anything but my own opinion of the matter. I am much inclined to think that this step of the two Imperialist Ministers is only an attempt to bully, and that, if it fails, as it seems hitherto to have done, it will be disavowed or retracted by their Governments. But then it seems to me that the only way

[1] Canning to Palmerston, Oct. 5th, 1849. Art. 11 of the Treaty of Kainardji expressly excepts from its reach "*ceux qui dans l'Empire de Russie auront embrassé la religion Chrétienne, et dans l'Empire Ottoman la religion Mahométane.*"

of bringing about that result is to give the Sultan the cordial and firm support of England and France, and to let the two Governments of Russia and Austria see that the Turk has friends who will back him and defend him in time of need. This might be done, first, by firm though friendly representations at Vienna and St Petersburg, pointing out that the Sultan is not bound by treaty to do what has been required, and that, not being so bound, he could not have done it without dishonour. Secondly, we might order our respective squadrons in the Mediterranean to take post at the Dardanelles, and to be ready to go up to Constantinople if invited by the Sultan, either to defend Constantinople from actual or threatened attack, or to give him that moral support which their presence in the Bosphorus would afford. I feel the most perfect conviction that Austria and Russia would not, in the present state of Germany, Poland, and Northern Italy, to say nothing of only half-pacified Hungary, venture upon a rupture with England, France and Turkey upon such a question as this. But all this is only my own personal opinion, and I cannot answer for the Broadbrims of the Cabinet; therefore do not, before you hear from me again, commit the Government to any opinion or to any course of action[1].

Canning's despatches arrived on October 1st, on which day also Palmerston received from Mehmed Pasha, Turkish Minister at St James', the official request of the Porte for moral and material aid from England in case of necessity[2]. Within twenty-four hours, the Cabinet had taken its decision (we hear

[1] Palmerston to Normanby, Sept. 29th, 1849, in Ashley, vol. II. pp. 107–8.
[2] Mehmed Pasha to Palmerston, Oct. 1st, 1849. *Refugees*, No. 15.

no more of the "Broadbrims") and a private letter
was immediately despatched to Canning: England
had decided to support Turkey morally and materially, and to induce France to cooperate in whatever
measures might be taken. Friendly and courteous
representations were to be made at Vienna and St
Petersburg in support of the Sultan's decision with
respect to the refugees; and, at the same time, the
French and English Mediterranean squadrons were
to proceed to the Dardanelles with orders to go up
to Constantinople if invited to do so by the Sultan,
either to defend his capital from attack or to give
him the moral support which their presence would
afford.

"I think it, however, much better," Palmerston continues, "that the Porte should be advised *not* to send
for the squadron to enter the Dardanelles without real
necessity. The example might be turned to bad account
by the Russians hereafter; and it would be too much of
an open menace, and the way to deal with the Emperor
is not to put him on his mettle by open and public
menace. The presence of the squadrons at the outside
of the Dardanelles or in their neighbourhood would probably be quite sufficient to keep the Sevastopol squadron
at anchor in port...what I wish you to impress upon the
Turks is that this communication is confidential, to keep
up their spirits and courage; but that they must not
swagger upon it, nor make it public till they hear it
officially[1]."

On October 6th the official despatches were written.

[1] Palmerston to Canning, Oct. 2nd, 1849, in Lane-Poole,
op. cit. vol. II. p. 197.

Once again, Palmerston urged great caution, and stated that the Porte must not be led out of the paths of prudence by the appearance of support:

It is essentially necessary that, in order to continue to receive the support of Great Britain, the Turkish Government should continue throughout, to be, as it has hitherto been, in the right in these affairs.

Once again, also, the Foreign Secretary sent an admonition that the squadrons should not appear within the Dardanelles without a real necessity; but the decision must of course rest with those who were on the spot[1]. On the 18th Canning received the confidential letter, and on the 24th the official despatch. On October 6th, too, Palmerston had written to Ponsonby at Vienna, to Bloomfield at St Petersburg and, also, to the Admiralty, instructing the Lords Commissioners to send the necessary orders to Sir William Parker. The latter was to take his squadron to the Black Sea, if necessary, but was to bear in mind that his task was defensive and not offensive, and that " consequently, wherever he may be, he should confine himself to the defence of Turkey, and should not undertake any offensive operations against the Russian territory or fleet." He was empowered to lend English officers, if Turkey requested, to assist in organising and manœuvring the Turkish fleet. Should the Turkish Government try to evade a crisis by assisting the chief refugees to leave its territory—which Palmerston personally

[1] Palmerston to Canning, Oct. 6th, 1849, *Refugees*, No. 18 (extract).

believed would be the best solution of the question—Sir William was authorised to offer the ships under his command for the purpose. The Vice-Admiral received these orders on October 17th, and on October 28th cast anchor in Besika Bay, outside the Straits of the Dardanelles[1].

The state of affairs in the early days of October is best seen in Palmerston's private letter to Bloomfield, which accompanied the official despatch:

We have endeavoured to make our despatch about the Poles as civil as possible, in order not to afford the Russian Government any pretext for saying that they have been threatened, and cannot in honour give way; and in my conversation with Brunnow and Colloredo[2] I have carefully abstained from saying anything about our squadron being ordered to the Dardanelles, or as to what we should do, if the Emperor persisted in his demand, and took hostile measures against Turkey to enforce it. But we have taken our resolution to support Turkey "*materiellement*" as well as "*moralement*." I hope, however, that the good sense of the Russian Government will save us from the very unpleasant task which would in that case devolve upon us.—The Sultan has clearly right upon his

[1] Palmerston to Bloomfield, Ponsonby and the Lords Commissioners of the Admiralty, Oct. 6th, 1849, *Refugees*, Nos. 19, 20, and 22. For a fuller text of the instructions to the Admiralty (which has been utilised above), see Vice-Admiral Augustus Phillimore, *Life of Sir William Parker* (London, 1876–80, 3 vols.), vol. III. pp. 564–5. This *Life* is a labour of love, extending over something upwards of 2000 pages; but Parker is a pleasant subject to read about even at such length. He was the last link with Nelson, and, like Sir Stratford, whatever he might be at home, was a good Radical abroad.

[2] The Russian and Austrian representatives in London.

side. That is the universal opinion of all men of all
parties, and of all newspapers in this country. There is
perfect unanimity on this point; and Brunnow and
Colloredo form no exception to this, for, though I beg
they may not be quoted, they both acknowledge that
the Sultan is not bound to give up the refugees. Colloredo
admits that the Austrian Treaty contains no stipulation
for surrender of refugees; and Brunnow says not only
that the Russian Treaty gives each party the choice of
expulsion instead of surrender, but he contends that this
choice was inserted by the Russian negotiators, expressly
because at that time more Turks fled to Russia than
Russians to Turkey, and the Russians did not wish to be
obliged to hand such refugees over to the certainty of
the bowstring. He told me he should write to Nesselrode
by last Friday's (yesterday's) post to this effect.—We
hope and trust that no war will come out of this question;
but if they hold high language to you and talk big about
war, bear in mind that we have made up our minds to
support Turkey by arms as well as by the pen. But keep
this in the background, unless absolutely forced to allude
to it.—You will of course give us the earliest information
of the course likely to be taken by the Russian Government, and of any military or naval measures which they
may contemplate. I do not myself think that they would
in any case make an attempt on Constantinople. It is
more likely that they would try to hold the Danube
Provinces as hostages for the Poles; but that could not
be allowed, and Austria would probably soon come over
to our side on such a question as that—at least unless
she has quite forgotten her traditionary policy in regard
to Turkey, blinded by furious rancour against the Hungarians[1].

[1] Palmerston to Bloomfield, Oct. 6th, 1849. Private letter.
Bloomfield Papers (in F. O. records at Chancery Lane).

Never before had there been such unanimity in England on a question only indirectly affecting this island; no Cabinet, whatever its politics, could have afforded for a single hour to leave its decision in doubt. Nor did Palmerston—although making every preparation for a European war—believe that the Czar would drive matters to an extremity. The latter was very much out of humour at what had been passing in Hungary since Világos, and the treatment meted out by the Austrians to his prisoners in that land. The war he had just finished had proved (English and French agents in Russia speak as one man on the point) very unpopular with his subjects. It had cost 84 millions of francs, and had brought in nothing. He might indeed order a levy of twelve men in every thousand—larger than any that had been seen since the *Grande Armée* invaded the Russian dominions, and the fleet at Sevastopol might have steam up night and day; but, as usual, the Russians were playing a game of bluff, and most of their boasted reserves of bullion were fabulous. Nicholas, although never tired of reiterating that the Turkish Empire was dead, was not prepared to hold stormy obituary rites in the autumn of 1849, and told the Princess of Würtemberg as much in so many words. The story reached the ears of Lord Cowley, English Minister at Frankfort, who promptly despatched it to Downing Street[1]. Austria might

[1] Lord Cowley to Palmerston, Oct. 9th, 1849 (private), also Colonel du Plat to Sir Stratford Canning, enclosed in a despatch of Canning to Palmerston, Oct. 21st (private and confidential).

wish to go further; but then Austria did not matter if one could be sure of Russia. So early as October 2nd Ponsonby had written that, on the part of Austria, nothing worse would happen than expressions of dissatisfaction; that no strong measures would be taken, and that the conduct of Titoff and the Internuncio was already being spoken of as precipitate[1].

Canning wrote home that there were moments when he found Aupick inclined to stimulate rather than to follow him (which latter was the Frenchman's usual function), in the delicate and dangerous work which both diplomats had undertaken with no other instructions than the dictates of humanity and considerations of the Balance of Power. Such was not the case in London and Paris. The Roman affair was still pending, and the last thing the French Government wished for was a rupture with the Czar, so recently grown gracious to his "good friend" of France. "Don't be uneasy," the French representatives were wont to comfort their Austrian and Russian colleagues by saying; "*nous avons bien une politique à nous.*" On the first day of October, de Tocqueville sent a private letter to Drouyn de Lhuys in London. In the present crisis, he wrote, the action of England would have the greatest influence on France. Therefore, the English Cabinet must be asked clearly *how far* it was willing to go. "If they want us to assist them, they must dot their i's." Drouyn was, also, to learn the views of every shade

[1] Ponsonby to Palmerston, Oct. 2nd, 1849, *Refugees*, No. 25.

of Tory, for from England (commented the French Minister) the support of the party in power was not always a sufficient guarantee[1].

When the resolutions of the English Cabinet finally arrived, they more than disconcerted de Tocqueville; England risked her fleet only, but France would stake her "very existence" on such a move. The Assembly would certainly abandon the Ministers, if it came to a war. De Tocqueville accordingly, by his own confession, attended the Council which had been convoked to discuss the English propositions, resolved to oppose what had so bellicose a sound in them. To his surprise, he found Louis Napoleon already pledged, and in a moment of heat asserted that the English ambassador, Lord Normanby, had cajoled the Prince-President's mistress, Miss Howard. Long afterwards, he confessed to Nassau Senior that he had been mistaken; Normanby was not on good terms with Napoleon at the time[2]. The President was doubtless chiefly influenced by the regard for public opinion at home, and the dread of English preponderance at Constantinople, where the French had commercial and political interests equal to our own. He, too, doubtless knew that the Czar would not

[1] De Tocqueville, *Recollections*, p. 366. Bapst, *op. cit.* p. 92. De Tocqueville had not forgotten Palmerston's attitude in July. In that month he had written to Boislecomte, the French agent at Turin, that France would defend Piedmont if the Austrians attacked that country. When Palmerston heard this, he told Drouyn de Lhuys that England would not lend more than a diplomatic and moral support to Piedmont.

[2] De Tocqueville, *Recollections*, pp. 367–8; Marcel, *Essai Politique*, p. 413.

appeal to the ultimate argument of potentates. Lord Normanby did not fail to point out, moreover, to the French Government, that a real danger of war would be created if the Austrians and Russians suspected that there was not absolute unanimity between England and France. On October 9th, as de Tocqueville wrote to his friend Beaumont at Vienna, the Council was still "divided and perplexed." Molé, Thiers, Broglie—almost all the chiefs of the majority in the Chamber—held that it would be a mistake to engage in war for the refugees. But the President was

ardently for the adventure. I think that the step is premature, that we should not allow ourselves to be engaged otherwise and more than we wish, by a foreign nation which risks nothing, while we risk all[1].

The next day, Louis Napoleon was victorious, and the Council decided that the French fleet should be ordered by telegraph to put to sea immediately, to bear up towards Smyrna, and put itself into communication with Sir William Parker[2]. After this, the French diplomats at Vienna and St Petersburg needed every ounce of tact they possessed.

It is necessary to be on very good terms with the English Embassy, and yet not display an intimacy which could not fail to be harmful to you and the success of your negotiation; for Lord Palmerston is the *bête noire* of Prince Schwarzenberg. Doubtless you know that already.

[1] De Tocqueville to A. G. de Beaumont, Oct. 9th, in Marcel, *op. cit.* pp. 500–1.
[2] Lord Normanby to Palmerston, Oct. 11th, 1849 (secret), *Refugees*, No. 30. (A very colourless extract only.)

This is a matter of tact and address, respecting which we cannot give directions from a distance. For the rest I rely upon you. But the thing is to emphasize and bring out our firm desire, while saving the refugees, to prevent Turkey from becoming a receptacle for political refugees and a hearth of revolution[1].

Of course, nothing of all this was laid on the table of the House, and the world at large never suspected what the "absolute unanimity" and "cordial co-operation" of the two Western Powers in the autumn of 1849 really meant. "During the negotiations which took place at Constantinople," said Palmerston, in a speech in the Commons, "the most perfect harmony and cooperation existed between H.M. Ambassador and the Ambassador of the Republic of France[2]"; which was undoubtedly true.

Meanwhile, Fuad Effendi, after being cheered by du Plat at Warsaw, had arrived at St Petersburg on October 5th. Very soon after his arrival the British Chargé d'Affaires saw him, and gave him what presumably—for Buchanan had received no instructions as yet—were the views of the Government on the subject of the Polish refugees. On the 8th, the Turk had an interview with Count Nesselrode, who told him that the matter was susceptible of arrangement, but that all depended on the Czar's decision; the next day he was given to understand that "if Foreign Powers pretended to interfere in

---

[1] De Tocqueville to A. G. de Beaumont, Oct. 12th, 1849.
[2] Debate on Lord Dudley Stuart's Motion for Papers respecting the Refugees, Feb. 7th, 1850, Hansard, cviii. pp. 480–518.

the question at issue, His Imperial Majesty would
not listen to any terms of accommodation whatever[1]."
Finally, Fuad, after a discouraging term of suspense,
during which the English agent offered him a copy
of the *Times*, that he might see how the whole of
England was behind him, was granted an audience
with the Czar on October 16th, who, *more suo*, was
at first very haughty, but afterwards more placable.
That same evening the Czar told Count Nesselrode
that he gave up the claim of extradition, and that
normal diplomatic relations with the Porte were to
be established as soon as possible. The next day,
this news was communicated by the Chancellor to
Fuad. When Bloomfield asked for a copy of this
communication, Nesselrode refused, *"because he
could never admit the principle of foreign interference
in the relations of Russia with Turkey[2]."*

Palmerston, on hearing the news from St Petersburg, wrote to Canning in great glee:

All things have turned out well. The English Government and nation have shown a spirit, a generosity, a
courage which does us all high honour. We have drawn

[1] Buchanan to Palmerston, Oct. 10th and 12th, 1849.
Lord Bloomfield to Palmerston, Oct. 16th, *Refugees*, No. 44,
Bapst, p. 107. De Tocqueville says (*Recollections*, p. 373) that
Fuad refused to see anyone until he had seen Nicholas. This
is incorrect. Fuad did not see the French representative
Lamoricière, who was not a favourite in St Petersburg, and
whose whole behaviour, in spite of the eulogy of his biographer,
Keller, at this time was somewhat indiscreet. Bapst suggests
(p. 104) that du Plat had warned Fuad against the Frenchman.
See also Buchanan to Palmerston, Oct. 9th, *Refugees*, No. 88.
[2] Bloomfield to Palmerston, Oct. 19th, *Refugees*, No. 48;
and *Journal de Pétersbourg*, Oct. 7th–19th.

France to follow in our wake, after much division and difference of opinion in the French Cabinet and public. We have forced the haughty autocrat to go back from his arrogant pretensions; we have obliged Austria to forego another opportunity of quaffing her bowl of blood; and we have saved Turkey from being humbled down to absolute prostration. All this will be seen and felt by Europe; all this should be borne in mind by ourselves, and ought to be treasured up in grateful remembrance by Turkey; but all this *we* ought not to boast of, and, on the contrary, we must let our baffled Emperors pass as quietly and as decently as possible over the bridge by which they are going to retreat[1].

Both at St Petersburg and Vienna, the Turkish agents were, indeed, willing to grant more than Canning and Bloomfield thought should be granted. The vast majority of the refugees (about three thousand three hundred of the rank and file) accepted the Austrian offers of amnesty, and returned to Austrian territory. As regards the principal refugees who were Austrian subjects, the Ottoman Minister at Vienna, Musurus, acting on his own responsibility, undertook not only to *"interner et surveiller"* them in the interior of the Empire, but promised that the measure *"ne cesserait qu'après une entente préalable avec le Cabinet de Vienne."* Ponsonby saw nothing objectionable in the engagement, and it was this which so roused Palmerston's ire against the ambassador that he wrote the letter which has already been quoted in extracts earlier in this essay. Canning, of

[1] Palmerston to Canning, Oct. 28th, 1849. (Of course, a private letter.) In Lane-Poole, vol. II. p. 202.

course, saw much that was objectionable in the promise, and set to work at once to obtain the correction of a "real blot" on the final settlement of the question[1]. The Czar, on the other hand, demanded, in the first place, the expulsion of all Russian subjects who had fled across the Danube, whatever their passports might be; secondly, the Porte must come to an arrangement with other Powers in whose dominions Polish subjects had been naturalised without the Czar's consent, to expel any such if they should appear in Turkey and engage in intrigues against Russia; lastly, the Porte was to send away into the interior of Asia Minor those prominent refugees whose extradition the Czar had demanded, but who had embraced the faith of Islam. Of these demands, as Palmerston pointed out, the second it was not within the competence of the Porte to grant, while the third was distinctly at variance with those very treaty stipulations upon which the Russians had originally based their claim.

It would have been better to send away out of the country all the refugees without distinction; however, the Porte had tied its hands, if not by the proceedings of Fuad and Musurus at St Petersburg and Vienna respectively, at least by the terms of the Sultan's letter to the Czar, and of Aali's note of September 16th to Stürmer. If the Turks, wrote Palmerston, had fettered themselves by insufficiently considered

[1] Ponsonby to Palmerston, Oct. 23rd and Nov. 20th. Canning to Palmerston, Nov. 3rd. None of the relevant despatches was laid before Parliament.

communications, there must be no breach of positive pledges[1].

Meanwhile, new cause for friction had arisen in the action of the English fleet. When it was first known in St Petersburg and Vienna that Sir William Parker was sailing eastwards, the Russians and Austrians had declared that they could not retire in the face of a menace. To which it was replied that, if the Mediterranean squadron chose to exercise in the Levant or Archipelago, it was still in its proper sphere, and there was no suggestion of menace. On October 28th, as already related, the Vice-Admiral had anchored in Besika Bay, which is on the Asiatic coast, south of the Dardanelles. A fortnight before he arrived the immediate reception of his squadron in the Dardanelles, and even its passage into the Sea of Marmora, had been provided for by a secret order of the Porte to the Pasha of the Straits[2]. This order, of course, was only to be utilised in an extreme case. But the winter season was coming on; Besika Bay was an exposed place, and its bottom entirely unsuitable for anchorage; moreover, Sir William had had to contend with a heavy gale on his late journey from the Grecian Isles. When, therefore, the English

[1] Lord Bloomfield to Palmerston, Oct. 19th; Canning to Palmerston, Nov. 5th, 7th, and 12th. Palmerston to Canning, Nov. 30th. The relevant passages were not printed in the Whitebook, because it was not desirable that it should be known, either in or out of England, how much "foreign mediation" there had been in a matter which lay between the Porte on the one hand, and Russia and Austria on the other.

[2] Canning to Parker, Oct. 15th, in Phillimore, vol. III. p. 562.

vice-consul at the Dardanelles, Mr Calvert, told him that according to the existing general regulations of 1845 he was at liberty to pass the Outer Castles and enter the Straits proper, Parker decided to take advantage of the permission so soon as the weather was favourable to such an operation.

"Although some cavil might possibly be raised, or jealousy excited by your reception there," wrote Canning, on the last day of October, "I conceive that no such ground of objection can be expected to outweigh the advantages, essential as they are, of a sheltered anchorage and an easy approach to Constantinople[1]."

On November 1st Sir William, expecting fresh gales, left Besika Bay, and proceeded to pass the Outer Castles. Even while he was doing so, a sudden squall sprang up, and caused two of his weather-beaten vessels to run foul of each other. On November 3rd, as has been seen, Canning heard that the Austrians had given up the demand for extradition. Titoff and the Internuncio had already murmured that the Treaty of 1841 did not allow vessels of war to enter the Straits, and they would be sure to make the most of a peccadillo on the part of Downing Street. The regulations by virtue of which the squadron had passed the Outer Castles, ran as follows:

Vessels-of-war of all nations arriving in these Straits, without the necessary permission for their passage onwards having been received from Constantinople, are allowed to make choice of any anchorage between the Outer Castles and Point Nagara which the respective

[1] Canning to Palmerston, Oct. 31st, 1849.

commanders may consider the most convenient or safe, and where they will be required to remain until the arrival of a firman for them to pass on to Constantinople[1].

Sir William had, certainly, not infringed the letter of this clause, but there appeared to be little doubt that the vessels referred to were—as Palmerston wrote afterwards—

such light ships of war as, under the stipulations of the Treaty above mentioned, the Porte reserves to itself the right of permitting to pass the two Straits for the purpose of communicating with Foreign Embassies and Missions at Constantinople[2].

In times of peace, the paragraph was too narrow to cover a powerful squadron of line of battleships. The present moment, just when the West, recruited by an enlightened *Zeitgeist* and the spirit rather than the letter of the law, was winning a great victory over reaction and the lust for revenge, was no time for England to be caught in the slightest deviation from the paths of diplomatic rectitude. The Treaty of July 13th, 1841, which was intended as an eternal safeguard of Turkish independence, was the gospel of English diplomacy in the Near East; the independence of Turkey must never be purchased by an infringement of that document. Apart from the ethics of the case, there was, likewise, a strong motive of interest which ought to make England very scrupulous in the observance of the Treaty, for

[1] Calvert to Vice-Admiral Sir W. Parker, Oct. 26th, *Refugees*, No. 65 (Inclosure 2).
[2] Palmerston to Canning, Nov. 24th, *Refugees*, No. 75.

Russia would readily follow any example of its violation; and Russia, as Palmerston sagely remarked, would have more occasion to enter the Bosphorus than another Power to enter the Dardanelles, and could thence "directly and imminently threaten the Turkish Capital[1]." Information as to what was the Foreign Secretary's view of the matter did not reach the embassy at Therapia until all was over. Canning, in the early days of November, thought and continued to think that there was no infringement of the Treaty; but he did not wish to imperil the half-attained success.

"I conceive," he wrote to Parker on the 4th, "that the continuance of H.M. Squadron at its present anchorage can no longer be a matter of immediate urgency, and I only wish to ascertain the wishes of the Turkish Government in that respect before I submit the expediency of its removal to your consideration."

On the 7th, he knew that both Austria and Russia had given up their original demands, and became more pressing:

Under present circumstances I think it of real importance that you should take the squadron outside. My promise against its exposure to weather in a less sheltered situation supposed the prospect of a downright danger, which is probably more than you see reason to apprehend at either of the two nearest stations. Anxious for your comfort, I am sorry for the change[2].

[1] Palmerston to Canning, Nov. 30th, 1849. The passage quoted is omitted in the Whitebook.

[2] *Life of Parker*, vol. III. pp. 579–80.

But gales were still blowing, and prudence forbade
an attempt to leave the Straits at once; nor did
the winds become sufficiently moderate to admit of
retirement to Besika Bay until November 16th[1].
The legend grew up that the storm was merely an
invention of Palmerston and Canning. Sir Theodore
Martin writes in that sense; "*on prétexta une tempête*,"
say the French historians[2]. The truth is, Sir Stratford
Canning certainly wanted the fleet inside the Straits,
and had made the necessary arrangements with the
Porte before Parker had left Greek waters. But a
sailor's consideration for the safety of his ships in the
teeth of an actual formidable gale was the real reason
why the squadron entered the Straits: of that no
reader of the correspondence in Phillimore's biography can entertain any doubt. Fictitious winds
do not cause ships to run foul of each other, nor do
anchors drag in tranquil summer seas. Moreover,
had there been no storm, Parker would not have
stayed in the Straits during almost a fortnight after
receiving a request from Canning to repass the Outer
Castles as soon as possible.

It has, also, been asserted that the appearance of
the squadron in the Dardanelles nearly upset all that
had been gained at the last moment. This, too, is an
exaggeration. When the Russians knew that the
fleet was moving eastwards, they, indeed, declared,
as they had so often before, that they could not

---

[1] *Life of Parker*, vol. III. pp. 581–4.
[2] *Life of the Prince Consort*, vol. II. p. 242; *Le Général de
Lamoricière*, par E. Keller, vol. II. p. 221.

retire before a menace. But later, when it was known that the fleet was actually in the Dardanelles, Nesselrode seemed satisfied with the explanation[1]. And, when Bloomfield communicated to them Palmerston's disapproval of the interpretation given at Constantinople to the regulations concerning the Straits, it acted, wrote the Ambassador, "like a charm upon my relations, as well as those of my countrymen, with the Court." For many weary weeks not only the English Legation, but obscure English residents and travellers in St Petersburg, had been placed beyond the pale of imperial favours —so much so, indeed, that Bloomfield would fain have had recourse to diplomatic reprisals, but was prevented by Palmerston's common-sense.

Schwarzenberg sent a protest against the entry of the fleet into the Straits, which was communicated to Palmerston on December 4th. Nesselrode sent a despatch—not a formal protest—which Baron Brunnow was to communicate to Palmerston; it expresses entire satisfaction with the Foreign Secretary's admission that a forced interpretation had been given to the Treaty of 1841 at Constantinople, and with his engagement that the obligations of that treaty should be more strictly observed in the future[2]. Palmerston could not refrain from the joy of replying to Schwarzenberg, and, on the first day of 1850, sent

[1] Bloomfield to Palmerston, Nov. 15th, 1849; and private letter, Dec. 28th, 1849.

[2] Baron Koller to Palmerston, Dec. 4th, 1849; Baron Brunnow to Palmerston, Jan. 2nd, 1850: *Refugees*, Nos. 87 and 109.

a despatch to Ponsonby, which stated that, although
the Government would not go back on what they
had already said as to the entrance of the fleet into
the Dardanelles, yet it might very well be argued
that that entrance was, after all, not contrary to the
Port regulations of 1845. And, since the Treaty of
1841, also, recorded the determination of the five
signatory Powers to respect and to uphold the
independence of the Porte, the appearance of the
squadron in the Dardanelles, "even if it was an infringement, was at all events not the first infringement
of that Treaty." Moreover, the Clause excluding ships
of war applied only when the Porte should be really
and substantially at peace; but could a condition of
things be honestly called peace, when the Austrian
and Russian agents at Constantinople had declared
that the escape of a single refugee meant war?

If the Sultan threatened in so peremptory a manner by
the official organs of two Great Powers immediately
adjoining to his frontiers, had actually invited into the
heart of his Empire the armed assistance of friendly
allies to protect him against a formidable danger, the
outbreak of which was made to depend upon a contingency which he might be unable to prevent, it is not the
Government of Austria that could with any degree of
consistency have objected to the general principle upon
which such an invitation would have been founded[1].

The French Government had from the first acted
very unwillingly in despatching their fleet (which,
by the way, did not enter the Dardanelles), to join

[1] Palmerston to Ponsonby, Jan. 1st, 1850, *Refugees*, No. 103.

Parker's squadron, and very soon began to agitate for the recall of the combined squadron. Palmerston, however, waited until he had reason to believe that the chief differences between the Porte and the Imperial Governments had been settled; and not until the last week of November did he write to Constantinople that Parker was to retire to his accustomed station, whenever Canning should deem it safe and prudent. He (Canning) was to act in conjunction with General Aupick[1]. But, although the main difficulty had been surmounted, Austria and Russia still demanded that which Canning thought an independent Government should never grant, and he still persisted in the arduous labour of keeping the Porte up to the necessary degree of firmness. Finally, Russia accepted the Turkish modifications of her three original demands, but insisted that the agreement should be drawn up in a formal Protocol. The Protocol was signed on Christmas Day, and distinctly states that the measures to be executed were adopted by common consent; Russia was thus placed on the same footing as Turkey in a matter falling within the exclusive competency of the Porte. Canning, of course, deplored such ill-timed compliance, but heartily desired to see the affair settled. "The most useful and best intentioned interference," he wrote wearily, "has its limits. Ours, I conceive, has reached them under the present circumstances." On the last day but one of the old year, Titoff resumed diplomatic relations with the Porte, and Canning

[1] Palmerston to Canning, Nov. 24th, 1849, *Refugees*, No. 76.

thought that he might safely inform Parker that his presence on the Turkish side of the Archipelago was no longer necessary. The official "liberty to quit" was forwarded on the first day of 1850[1].

Schwarzenberg was far more *intransigeant* than the Czar, and still insisted on those points which the Turks at Constantinople declared they could not accept, but which the Austrians declared had already been consented to by Musurus at Vienna: the confinement and surveillance of the refugees was only to cease with the mutual consent of Austria and the Porte; the list of such refugees was to be kept open for the inclusion of new names; and an Austrian commissary was to be sent to Kutaieh, the town in Asia Minor agreed upon as the locality of confinement, to observe how the insurgent chiefs were being guarded. These demands, pressed forward with more than Roman arrogance, would have made the chief of the Mahometans Schwarzenberg's turnkey. Palmerston was not behind Canning in his condemnation of such preposterous articles. "It is scarcely less derogatory to the Sultan," he wrote, "to be jailor for Austria than to be purveyor to the Austrian executioners[2]." Week after week, the weary negotiations dragged on, and very slowly the Austrians

---

[1] Canning to Palmerston, Dec. 18th, Dec. 24th, Dec. 26th, Dec. 31st, *Refugees*, Nos. 110 (extract), 113 (extract) and 115.

[2] Quoted in Lane-Poole, *op. cit.* vol. II. p. 204. The history of the Refugees during 1850–1 may be traced in the second Whitebook, *Further Correspondence respecting Refugees from Hungary*, presented to the House of Lords by command of Her Majesty, June, 1852.

abated their pretensions; not until a large part of the New Year had gone did Francis Joseph finally give way, and diplomatic relations with the Porte were not finally renewed till the first week of April. But a weary term of confinement still lay before the refugees, for the Sultan, though he had saved them and defied the Austrian Government, was still possessed of a wholesome fear of that Government's ire. Sir Stratford Canning still laboured ceaselessly in their interests, and finally obtained the Sultan's promise that they should be released in September 1851. At that date the men who had held the chanceries of the East and West in suspense for so many weeks and almost caused a universal war, left Turkish territory for ever. The man who had saved these "miserable relicts of a lost cause" was Palmerston, who had declared, again and again, that he knew nothing of a sovereign independent Hungary.

INDEX

For EU product safety concerns, contact us at Calle de José Abascal, 56–1°,
28003 Madrid, Spain or eugpsr@cambridge.org.